Be
Alaska

Text: Nancy Gates
Managing Editor: Clare Peel
Series Editor: Tony Halliday

Berlitz POCKET GUIDE

Alaska

First Edition 2006

PHOTOGRAPHY CREDITS

ADF&G/Alaska Division of Community and Business Development 85; Alaska Department of Commerce, Community, and Economic Development 6; Alaska Division of Community and Business Development 2TR, 22, 27, 100, 101; Alaska Division of Tourism 2CL, 3, 11, 14, 26, 29, 31, 34, 38, 39, 41, 47, 48, 53, 55, 57, 58, 59, 60, 67, 70, 73, 75, 76, 77, 81, 82, 86, 89, 91, 98; Alaska Division of Tourism/Robert Angell 1, 2BR, 9/Robin Hood 7, 13, 32, 37/John Hyde 97/Mark Noble 51/ E. Sommer 63/Mark Wayne 93; Corbis 24; FCVB Archive 19, 94; Kevin Fleming/Corbis 42/43; Nome Visitors Centre 79; Hagerty Patrick/Corbis Sygma 69; Museum of History and Art 44; Juneau Convention and Visitors Bureau 35; University of Washington Libraries 16, 17, 20 Cover picture: courtesy Holland America Line

CONTACTING THE EDITORS

Every effort has been made to provide accurate information in this publication, but changes are inevitable. The publisher cannot be responsible for any resulting loss, inconvenience or injury. We would appreciate it if readers would call our attention to any errors or outdated information by contacting Berlitz Publishing, PO Box 7910, London SE1 1WE, England. Fax: (44) 20 7403 0290; e-mail: berlitz@apaguide.co.uk www.berlitzpublishing.com

Native Alaska art and culture are among the highlights of the gateway city of Ketchikan (page 26)

Spot sea lions in the fjords and inlets of mountain-backed Prince William Sound (page 52)

Try bear-watching in Katmai National Park and Preserve (page 62), near Kodiak Island

TOP TEN ATTRACTIONS

Out of this world – the Northern Lights (page 71), as seen from Fairbanks ▼

Fly-fishing is a popular activity on the Russian River (page 58) ◀

Anchorage (page 43) is Alaska's largest city and cultural heart ▶

Haines Bald Eagle Festival (page 39) celebrates an annual gathering of this noble bird ▶

Mount McKinley dominates Denali National Park (page 64) ▼

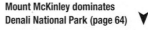

Natural grandeur – Kenai Fjords National Park (page 57) ▶

Kayak among icebergs at Glacier Bay National Park (page 36) ▶

CONTENTS

Fact Sheets

INTRODUCTION

Dreams of Alaska are the dreams of adventurers – those daring to cruise, fly, or climb out past the ordinary edge – to experience what lies beyond. Many will venture deep into the forest to watch breathlessly as massive brown bears grapple with salmon at the base of a waterfall. Most will keep a close eye out for moose browsing among birch and alder trees by the roadside, or even in the hotel parking lot. Some long to hear the sudden crack and thunderous roar of calving tidewater glaciers; others long for the solitude of hiking, kayaking, or river rafting in a backcountry adventure. Alaska is so vast, so diverse, so achingly beautiful it dwarfs preconceived notions. But adventurers should be forewarned: while the depth and breadth and grandeur of Alaska may outstrip your imagination, its accessibility and amenities, particularly in remote areas or during off-seasons, may prove more challenging than you expect.

The icy waters of Glacier Bay

Regions and Climate

By far the largest of the 50 states, Alaska's 586,412 sq miles (1,518,000 sq km) is one-fifth the size of the combined 'Lower 48' states. Alaska has 34,000 miles (54,700km) of shoreline (more than twice that of the rest of the country), 14 major mountain ranges, 17 of the nation's 20 highest peaks, 70 hot springs, at least 100 volcanoes and volcanic fields,

Totem poles are one of the most dramatic forms of Native art

100,000 glaciers, about 3,000 rivers, and millions of lakes. There are four main geographic areas.

Southeast Alaska (also known as the Panhandle) is a narrow strip of land sandwiched between the Pacific Ocean and Canada; numerous islands lie just offshore. The Southeast is covered by huge temperate rainforests nurtured by high rainfall and mild temperatures: summer highs of 60° or 70°F (15° or 21°C) are not uncommon, and in the winter the mercury does not often dip much below freezing.

Southcentral Alaska lies along the Gulf of Alaska. A region of mountains, fjords, glaciers, and forested lowlands, it includes Anchorage (Alaska's largest city), Prince William Sound, the Kenai Peninsula, Kodiak Island, and the Matanuska-Susitna Valley. Southcentral is the most populous part of the state. The mild climate is drier than the Southeast's.

Between the Brooks and Alaska mountain ranges lies the **Interior**. It includes the Yukon, Alaska's longest river, and the Denali Range, home of Mount McKinley,

> **Residents of Barrow, in the far north of the Bush, have continuous daylight for 84 days in summer; Barrow is without sun for 67 days during winter.**

North America's highest peak. Some areas are dominated by birch and spruce; others support only tundra. Temperatures can drop to below –50°F (–45°C) in winter and climb to 70–80°F (21–26°C) or higher in the summer.

Anything outside these three regions is known as the **Bush**, the most remote and least populated part of Alaska. Much of its far north lies within the Arctic Circle, and consists of tundra. Mid-summer temperatures may reach 80°F (26°C) or higher, while mid-winter temperatures may sink to –40°F (–40°C) or below. The southwest of the Bush, including Nome, the Alaska Peninsula, and the Aleutian Islands, has a milder climate, but temperatures in winter are still well below freezing.

Most of Alaska is bear country

Wildlife

More than a million visitors travel to Alaska each year to see the sights, especially the wildlife, first hand. The National Audubon Society records 462 naturally occurring bird species in Alaska. Millions of ducks, geese, swans, and seabirds flock to breeding grounds and nesting colonies along the Alaskan coast each year. Migratory birds come from every continent but Europe. Copper River Delta (near Cordova) is the site of one of the world's largest concentrations of shorebirds in May. Eagles are so ubiquitous they commonly dominate city landfills.

Polar, black, and brown bears, moose, caribou, Dall sheep, Sitka black-tailed deer, elk, mountain goats, bison, musk oxen, and wolves are among Alaska's large land mammals. Marine mammals include dolphins, walruses, porpoises, sea otters, seals, sea lions, and whales.

Of course, not everyone comes to Alaska to sightsee. The state's renowned big-game hunting and world-class sport

> The word 'Alaska' may come from the Aleut word *alaxsxag* or *agunalash*, which translates as 'great land' or 'where the sea breaks its back.'

fishing opportunities draw hunters and anglers from throughout the world.

Population

Alaska's 655,000 residents are as diverse as the land they inhabit. Almost half live within the Municipality of Anchorage, followed by the Fairbanks North Star Borough (85,000), and the City and Borough of Juneau, the capital (31,000). Alaska Native people make up about 16 percent of the population.

Life in Alaska's larger cities is similar to that in other US cities: suburban homes with heated garages, wireless internet, satellite TV, and cell phones, with museums and fine restaurants to visit. Yet, in the remote St Lawrence Island community of Gambell (population 648), Yup'ik whaling captains still prepare their walrus-skinned boats for traditional hunts on the Bering Sea. Alaskans live out their diverse lives on the edge of tomorrow, yet within the culturally rich remnant of the past.

Reality Check

While the superlatives of Alaska take flight, it's important to realize that this wilderness land takes little notice of the frailties of man. Visitors are sometimes surprised to learn that Alaska offers less than they expect. This is especially true for the independent traveler. Misconceptions regarding economical transportation options to and within the state, cost and availability of lodging, goods, and services in remote areas (or during off-season), and specific wildlife viewing expectations can cloud an otherwise outstanding trip.

Transportation to and within Alaska merits early and careful consideration. Don't plan on buying a bus ticket to

Alaska, as most bus trips are a part of a tour package. Likewise, there is no connection between the Alaskan and Canadian railway systems. Visitors may choose to travel by cruise ship, by air, by private vehicle via the Alaska Highway, or by ferry with the Alaska Marine Highway System (from Bellingham, Washington or Prince Rupert, British Columbia). Commercial airlines provide reliable, year-round service to major Alaskan cities.

Visitors will discover excellent public transportation in Alaska's larger cities. Tour operators offer access to popular destinations, but usually from mid-May until mid-September only. Car and RV rentals are available in major hubs, but only 100 of the 300 Alaskan communities are on the road system. Transportation options from larger cities to more remote areas by bus, train, ferry, or small plane are available – but perhaps not on a daily basis, and possibly just during

Alaska Native women sporting some furry fashion

Wildlife Viewing

Here are some suggestions to enhance your wildlife viewing potential:

• Timing is almost everything. Make sure you time your visit for the optimal season for the wildlife you hope to see. Wildlife sightings are generally best at dawn and dusk.

• Familiarity with the diet of specific animals will help you know where (and when) to look for them.

• Proper equipment (like binoculars or a spotting scope) will help you observe wildlife without getting too close. Money spent on quality equipment is an excellent investment for what may be a once-in-a-lifetime opportunity.

• Invisibility is your friend. Neutral colors and unscented cosmetics will help you keep a low profile while observing animals. So will patience, moving slowly, and being quiet.

• Careful observation will often yield clues: animal calls, scat, tracks, worn paths, and areas where vegetation has been chomped or flattened.

• Field guides from local authoritative sources will be helpful. The Alaska Department of Fish and Game's Wildlife Notebook Series and Alaska Wildlife Viewing Guide are excellent resources. Find out more at <www.wildlife.alaska.gov>.

• Questions are appropriate and encouraged if there's an on-site ranger, naturalist or other Alaska wildlife expert. The staff at any office of the Alaska Public Lands Information Centers (see Travel Tips, *pages 122–4*) is happy to answer inquiries, too.

Ethical Guidelines for Wildlife Viewing

• Harassment of wildlife (by calling, clapping, whistling, throwing stones) is stressful to the animals and illegal.

• Stay on designated trails, if possible. Do not disturb rookeries, nesting, and denning areas or calving grounds.

• Do not attempt to rescue 'orphaned' animals. The parents are probably watching.

certain seasons. The Alaska Marine Highway ferry system is an excellent (year-round) option for those independent travelers who wish to visit the various coastal communities in the Southeast and Southcentral and in the southwestern part of the Bush.

Wildlife is one of the major reasons people visit the state, but not all animals can be found in all areas. Polar bears only live on the arctic ice cap on the northern fringes of Alaska. Moose are most commonly found in the Southcentral and Interior regions. Some advance research will ensure that you travel to the part of Alaska, and the habitats of the animals, you hope to see.

Year-round options for food and lodging are plentiful in the larger cities but in demand during the tourist season. Availability of these services outside the populated areas is dramatically reduced – or unavailable. For example, it is not advisable to drive from Anchorage to Denali National Park on a whim, assuming you can book a room in a hotel when you arrive. The lodging options near the park entrance (both at hotels and campgrounds) are often fully booked months in advance, and there are very few alternatives close by. You may well have to drive 240 miles (386km) south to Anchorage, or 125 miles (200km) north to Fairbanks, for a night's lodging.

The float plane awaits

Regardless of the challenges, a journey to glimpse the majesty of Alaska is a rare gift. With careful planning, the experience will awaken your senses, rejuvenate your imagination, enlarge your horizons, and allow you to realize the kind of dreams only adventurers dare to dream.

A BRIEF HISTORY

No one is certain when or how people first arrived in Alaska. One theory is that starving Siberian hunters tracked game migrations across the then-exposed Siberian Land Bridge, traveling the length and breadth of the land, creating a variety of shelters, tools, and hunting techniques suited to the demands of their new environments. The first wave of hunters probably made their way to what is now Southeast Alaska and western Canada, and later became known as the Tlingit, Haida, and Tsimshian Indians. One tiny corner of today's Southcentral Alaska became the home of the Eyak people. These early northwest coastal Indians lived in relative leisure and wealth due to a mild climate and plentiful food sources.

Traditional Native footwear

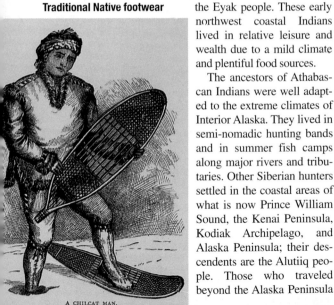

A CHILCAT MAN.
From a Drawing by Mrs. Willard.

he buckskin suit is trimmed with fur and quills. The narrow snow-shoe ed in hunting and running, and the broad one is used in

The ancestors of Athabascan Indians were well adapted to the extreme climates of Interior Alaska. They lived in semi-nomadic hunting bands and in summer fish camps along major rivers and tributaries. Other Siberian hunters settled in the coastal areas of what is now Prince William Sound, the Kenai Peninsula, Kodiak Archipelago, and Alaska Peninsula; their descendents are the Alutiiq people. Those who traveled beyond the Alaska Peninsula and down the Aleutian Chain were the forefathers of the Aleut. From the early 18th century the latter two cultures were heavily influenced by Russian religion and customs. Both peoples were excellent hunters, and derived most of their food and livelihood from the sea. Inuit (or Eskimo) groups are thought to have descended from the last wave of Alaska's first peoples. Today they are divided into three language groups: the Inupiat of the High Arctic, the Siberian Yupik of St Lawrence Island, and the Yup'ik and Cup'ik of southwest Alaska.

European Contact

In July of 1741 two Russian ships, the *St Paul* and *St Peter*, reached the shores of southern Alaska, though bad weather cut off communications between the vessels. Alexsei Chirikov, captain of the *St Paul*, sighted the islands of the Alaska panhandle and sent two landing parties ashore for fresh water. Both parties mysteriously disappeared, but the *St Paul* returned to Kamchatka in October. The *St Peter*, captained by Vitus Bering, ran aground in November on what is now called Bering Island. Bering and 20 of his crew died of scurvy on the island. The remaining 46 men survived the winter, built a ship out of the debris of the *St Peter* and returned to Kamchatka in the spring of 1742 loaded with treasure: sea-otter pelts.

Russian fur traders immediately headed for the Aleutians, with tragic results for the Aleut people: the traders enslaved them, splitting and relocating families. Eighty percent of the Aleut population was wiped out by violence and European disease within the first 100 years of Russian occupation.

Other nations took an interest in the North Pacific. British Captain James Cook, searching for the Northwest

> The Steller sea lion and Steller's jay owe their names to the field work of Georg Wilhelm Steller, a German naturalist aboard the ill-fated *St Peter* in 1741.

Captain James Cook

Passage, reached the inlet now named after him in May 1778. Cook eventually sailed to the Aleutians. He later died in Hawaii, but his crew sailed on to China, with a valuable cargo of sea-otter pelts. Interest in the Alaska fur trade grew throughout Europe.

Grigori Ivanovich Shelikov founded a permanent Russian settlement on Kodiak Island in 1784. He subdued the local Alutiiq people, constructed schools, and introduced the Russian Orthodox religion. In 1790 Alexander Baranov was hired to oversee Russia's fur trade. In 1799 he built a trading post and fort on what became Baranof Island. The settlement was eventually called Sitka and, by 1808, it had become the capital of Russian America.

By 1805, there had been some 200 European scientific and commercial voyages to Alaska. British navigator George Vancouver charted the Inside Passage (1791–95). The work of Spanish cartographers is still reflected in the names of various sites within Alaska. Competition for the fur trade increased dramatically with the establishment by the British of the Hudson Bay Company on the southern edge of Russian America, and by American hunters and trappers moving into the area. By the late 1850s, depletion of the sea-otter population, and relentless competition from Britain and American interests, led to a decline in Russian interest in Alaska. In 1866, Russia proposed selling their Alaska interests to the United States. A treaty ratified by the US Senate on May 27, 1867 purchased Alaska from Russia for $7.2 million – about 2 cents per acre.

From 1867–84, Alaska was without any real form of civil government. In 1884, the First Organic Act brought civil government, providing a district governor, appointed by the president, and public education. In 1906 Alaskans were allowed to send one non-voting member to the House of Representatives in Washington, DC. The Home Rule Act of 1912 granted Alaska territorial status and Alaskans were finally able to elect their own legislature.

Fur, Gold, and Mineral Rushes

With sea otters hunted nearly to extinction, the assets of the Russian America Company were sold to the San Francisco-based Alaska Commercial Company, and interest shifted to the plush coats of fur seals. The first of many 'rushes' began, and continued at such a frantic pace that by 1910 only a few thousand seals, out of an estimated three million, remained.

Prospectors arrive by sea

While dreams of the fur trade dwindled, visions of gold were on the horizon. Alaska's first major gold strike was in 1880, led by a French Canadian, Joe Juneau, and his partner, Richard Harris. The men struck pay dirt at Gold Creek in Southeast, and the mining town that grew from the strike was named Juneau. Major strikes in the Interior were at Forty-Mile River (on the Yukon border) in 1886, and at Circle in 1893.

George Washington Carmack and his Indian partners, Skookum Jim and Tagish Charlie, discovered gold in the Klondike (Canada's Yukon Territory) in 1896. Access to the Klondike gold fields was through the Alaska towns of Skagway and Dyea in Southeast. About 100,000 fortune hunters, most of them poorly prepared and sadly misinformed, attempted the treacherous trek over the Chilkoot Trail or White Pass with the requisite one-year's provisions. About 40,000 miners

Dishing the Dirt in Dawson

Mining was a laborious business, and those who went to the gold fields thinking the precious metal was there for the taking were soon disillusioned. The early prospectors had been lucky, striking gold near the surface, but by the time the influx of hopefuls reached Dawson in the Klondike they were digging for gold that could be 50ft (15m) below the surface. To reach it they had to force through permafrost, burning fires to soften the land, then sinking shafts which may, or may not, hit the right spot.

Once the 'pay dirt' – the mix of earth and gold – had been extracted it had to be separated and cleaned, and this was done in a primitive sluice. When the streams began to thaw in spring, water channeled through the sluice separated the precious dust from the dirt. The more sophisticated hydraulic sluicing methods introduced in Silver Bow could not be used in Dawson because of the difficulty of getting equipment across the passes.

A mining rocker, used for washing gold

completed the trip, and only a few realized the riches of their dreams. Others either turned back, discouraged, died from disease or other hardships along the trail, or spread out across Alaska to continue the search. Three Scandinavian prospectors discovered gold in 1898 along the Bering Sea at Cape Nome. Four years later an Italian by the name of Felix Pedro struck gold in the Tanana Valley. A trading post set up on the nearby Chena River became the city of Fairbanks.

Gold was not the only precious metal discovered. In 1900, prospectors along the Chitina River in the Wrangell-St Elias Mountains unearthed one of the world's largest copper reserves near the Kennicott Glacier.

World War II and its Aftermath

In 1940, Alaska experienced a different kind of 'rush.' World War II spurred the United States Government to consider the strategic importance of Alaska. Tens of thousands of people moved northward to Anchorage after Fort Richardson was established, and work began on Elmendorf Air Force Base. Supporting this large number of people was a challenge, and congressional appropriations for bases, airstrips, and housing grew rapidly. In February 1942, President Roosevelt authorized the Alaska Canada Military Highway, creating the first land route to Alaska and the Yukon from the Lower 48 states. Today, thousands drive cars, trucks, and RVs to Alaska each year along this same route, now widened and paved, and called the Alaska Highway.

World War II produced an economic boom in Alaska, adding over $1 billion of government money to the region, and doubling the population. During the Cold War and the Korean conflict, additional federal monies and military personnel arrived in Alaska. Today, more than 23,000 service members and 33,000 dependents are stationed here.

An earthquake hits Anchorage in 1964

Statehood

On January 3, 1959, nearly 100 years after its purchase from Russia, Alaska became the 49th state of the USA. The concerns of Native peoples about the ownership and use of traditional hunting, trapping, and fishing grounds grew, and the proposed construction of an oil pipeline eventually resulted in the Alaska Native Claims Settlement Act of 1971. Under this landmark act, Alaska Natives received $962.5 million in compensation, and title to 44 million acres (18 million hectares) of land (more than 10 percent of the state). Thirteen regional Native corporations were formed under this act to manage the money and land received from the government.

Just prior to this, in 1968, oil was discovered at Prudhoe Bay. The oil-field capacity was estimated at 10 billion barrels, the largest in the country. The Alyeska Pipeline Company was formed to build an 800-mile (1,290-km) pipeline from Prudhoe Bay, on the Beaufort Sea, to the Port of Valdez on Prince William Sound. Construction began in March 1975, and the first oil flowed in June 1977.

In 1980, Congress, under the leadership of President Jimmy Carter, enacted the Alaska National Interest Lands and Conservation Act (ANILCA). The passage of ANILCA established 10 new national parks within Alaska, enlarged existing national parks, and doubled the size of the US national park and refuge system. Addi-

One of the most enduring of the Alaska rushes is tourism. In 1890, some 5,000 visitors cruised the Inside Passage of Southeast Alaska by steamship. Native culture and art, the White Pass and Yukon Route narrow-gauge railroad, wildlife, spectacular scenery, and adventure attracted pioneer travelers then as they do today. In 2004, 1.4 million visitors came here by air, cruise ship, bus, or private vehicle.

The latest in pipeline technology

tional lands were designated as wildlife refuges, wilderness areas, national forests, national monuments, and wild rivers. A total of 131 million acres (53 million hectares) of Alaska was affected by this one act.

Alaska Today

Today, less than 1 percent of Alaska is privately owned – the remainder is state, federal, or Native Corporation owned property. Revenues from petroleum, mining, seafood, tourism, forest products, international air cargo, and other businesses have provided a stable state economy since statehood in 1959. Alaska's wealth of natural resources is in increasing demand, as new and more efficient technologies make it more accessible than ever. As the nation debates oil and gas exploration in the Arctic National Wildlife Refuge (ANWR), pro-development Alaskans support the idea as a means of reducing US dependence on foreign oil while creating jobs and economic growth. Preservationists feel it's vital to leave much of Alaska's wilderness completely untouched. Conservationists search for middle ground: responsible use of land for economic and recreational purposes that meets people's needs without sacrificing wildlife and beauty. The tension between these three polarized groups are the guide wires of Alaska's politics. The struggle is an important one: the economic and political benefit of accessing the vast natural resources of Alaska, versus the need to preserve and protect one of the last wild places on earth.

Historical Landmarks

1741–2 Russians arrive in Alaska and establish fur trade.

1778 James Cook visits Aleutians, arousing British interest in fur trade.

1784 Shelikof establishes Russian settlement on Kodiak Island.

1790 Baronof oversees Russian fur-trade interests in Alaska.

1791–5 George Vancouver charts the Inside Passage.

1867 Alaska purchased from Russia for $7.2 million.

1880 Gold strike at Gold Creek. The town of Juneau is founded.

1884 First Organic Act brings civil government to Alaska.

1886 Gold strike on Forty-Mile River.

1893 Gold strike at Circle.

1896 Klondike gold rush.

1898 Nome gold rush.

1902 Fairbanks gold rush.

1906 Non-voting representation first permitted in Washington, DC.

1912 Territorial Status granted by the Home Rule Act.

1923 Alaska Railroad completed.

1935 Matanuska Valley Colonization project.

1940 Military build-up in Alaska.

1942 Japan bombs Dutch Harbor and occupies Kiska and Attu Islands.

1959 Statehood; Alaska becomes the 49th state of the USA.

1964 Strongest earthquake ever recorded in North America hits Prince William Sound, with a magnitude of 9.2 on the Richter Scale.

1968 Oil discovered on North Slope.

1971 Alaska Native Claims Settlement Act.

1973 Construction of trans-Alaska pipeline authorized.

1976 Alaska Permanent Fund established to ensure long-term benefit.

1977 First oil flows through trans-Alaska pipeline.

1980 Alaska National Interest Lands Conservation Act.

1989 *Exxon Valdez* spills 11 million gallons (42 million liters) of oil into Prince William Sound, killing thousands of birds and mammals.

1990s The ecosystem of Prince William Sound largely recovers.

Early 2000s Tourism continues to grow, as does the conservation debate.

WHERE TO GO

Alaska is a land of great diversity. It is the largest state in the union, and among the most sparsely populated. Urban Alaska means Anchorage, Fairbanks and Juneau – the latter is the capital, but is much smaller than Anchorage. Rural Alaska comprises the villages and towns scattered throughout the state; while wilderness Alaska encompasses vast regions of relatively untouched ground. It is this untamed wilderness that beckons most travelers to the 49th state.

SOUTHEAST ALASKA: THE INSIDE PASSAGE

Lush rainforests, towering, moss-draped evergreens, spongy muskeg, mild temperatures, and rain, rain, rain... this is Alaska? The mild, maritime climate of Southeast Alaska is a delightful surprise to visitors who envisioned a desolate, frozen landscape – as long as they thought to bring quality rain gear with them.

The sprawling Tongass National Forest and some of the world's largest, most active glaciers form the backdrop for the logging, fishing, and mining cities and towns of Southeast Alaska. The land and coastal waters provide habitat for a wide variety of wildlife, including whales, sea lions, porpoises, seals, bears, Sitka black-tailed deer, wolves, mountain goats, bald eagles, seabirds, and more.

Of the Southeast communities, only Haines, Skagway and Hyder are accessible by road. Others, sprinkled along the waterways and islands of Alaska's panhandle, must be reached by air or sea. Local Tlingit, Haida and Tsimshian art and culture are shared with visitors arriving by cruise ship, commercial or private plane and via the Alaska Marine Highway System ferry.

Mount McKinley

Ketchikan

The first Alaska port of call for vessels headed north is the gateway city of **Ketchikan** (population 7,700). Originally a Tlingit fish camp, today the area is an industrial center and a major port of entry for Southeast Alaska. The Ketchikan economy is based on commercial fishing, fish processing, tourism, and timber. In the late 1800s, adventurers seeking gold, fur, or fish traveled up the Inside Passage, and stopped here for supplies and 'social opportunities.' Regular scheduled commercial airline flights, Alaska Marine Highway System ferries, and cruise ships provide access to the city today. Often referred to as Alaska's 'First City' or the 'Salmon Capital of the World,' Ketchikan resounds with echoes of bygone days of lumberjacks, gold miners, and canneries, richly seasoned with Native art and culture.

Creek Street in Ketchikan

The Southeast Alaska Discovery Center (open May 6– ept 27 daily 8am– 5pm; admission charge; winter Tues–Sat 10am–4.30pm; free) is a great place to start learning about the nature and history of Southeast Alaska, the Tongass National Forest, and the area's indigenous peoples. The center, operated by the USDA Forest Service, also has information on cabins, camping, bear viewing, wildlife, hunting, hiking, and fishing in the Tongass.

Downtown Ketchikan offers ample opportunities to shop, sip coffee, visit museums, and more, all within easy walking distance of the dock area. Walking tour maps, available from the **Ketchikan Visitors Bureau** (131 Front St on cruise ship dock; open May–Sept daily; winter Mon–Fri), will direct you past salmon-spawning creeks, a fish ladder, local parks, totem poles, and the city's unique 'stair streets.' **Creek Street** is a pedestrian walkway along Ketchikan Creek featuring small, colorful houses (some of which served as bordellos during gold-rush days) that now house restaurants, galleries, gift shops, and the **Dolly's House Museum** (open May–Sept daily 10am–10pm; admission charge). **The Great Alaska Lumberjack Show** (three shows daily May–Sept; admission charge) fea-

Totem Poles

Totem poles, some as high as 60ft (18m) tall, are among the most popular examples of northwest Native woodworking. Figures, or totems, on the poles are comparable to family crests and are used to tell a story, legend, or event. The totemic symbols are usually animals (bears, eagles, killer whales, etc.), and their significance lies in myth.

tures covered grandstand seating for log rolling, sawing, axe throwing, and various other lumberjack-style competitions.

The **Totem Heritage Center** (open May–Sept daily 8am–5pm; admission charge; Oct–April Mon–Fri 1–5pm; free) features a unique collection of original totem poles retrieved from abandoned Native villages. Other totems, and a Native community house, can be seen at **Totem Bight State Park** (a few miles north of downtown; free). Watch master carvers creating authentic totems at **Saxman Native Village** (open daily; free), 2½ miles (4km) south of downtown, a park with totems and a carving shed. Saxman Village also has Native dance and storytelling (admission charge) and a gift shop.

You can learn about a different type of salmon 'fry' and see a live bald eagle display at the **Deer Mountain Tribal Hatchery and Eagle Center** (open May–Sept daily 8am–4.30pm; admission charge; winter by appointment). A few miles south of the downtown area, at the **George Inlet Cannery**, there are tours that detail the history of the fishing industry in Ketchikan.

The sights of Ketchikan can be enjoyed on your own, or on various tours – walking, horse-drawn (or engine-powered) trolley, bus, jeep, kayak, bicycle, or semi-submersible vessel. Visiting nearby attractions, such as **Misty Fjords National Monument** *(see below)*, requires travel from Ketchikan by floatplane, helicopter, or boat.

Misty Fjords National Monument

Misty Fjords, 22 miles (35km) east of Ketchikan, is a wild, gloriously remote coastal ecosystem that can only be reached by floatplane, helicopter or boat. The Monument's fjords, steep sea cliffs, active glaciers, and natural canals encompass over 2 million acres (1 million hectares) within the Tongass National Forest. Adventure opportunities include kayaking, camping, hiking, photography, hunting, fishing, and boating. Nearly all wildlife common to Southeast can be found here. The USDA Forest Service maintains public use cabins in the area (reservations may be made at the Ketchikan office). Camping is allowed throughout, but there are no roads, established campsites, or grocery stores. Come prepared. For additional information, go to <www.fs.fed.us/r10/tongass>.

Boats in Wrangell Harbour

Wrangell

The city of Wrangell, 89 miles (143km) north of Ketchikan, on the northwest tip of Wrangell Island, near the mouth of the Stikine River, is a mining, logging, and fishing community. The population (about 2,000) reflects a mixture of Tlingit, Russian, British, and American influences.

The **James and Elsie Nolan Center** (open May–Sept Mon–Fri 10am to 5pm, Sat–Sun variable; winter Tues–Fri 1–5pm), near the city dock, is the place to begin your exploration. Within the center you'll find information on the various walking, bus, bicycle, boat, kayak, plane, and helicopter tour options at the **Visitor Center**, and learn about the city's colorful past at the **Wrangell Museum** (admission charge).

As a relatively new Alaskan tourist destination, Wrangell offers rare opportunities for wildlife, bird, and glacier viewing. It is 39 miles (62km) by boat from the actively calving **LeConte Glacier**, the southernmost tidewater glacier in North America.

At Petroglyph Beach State Historic Park, more than 50 petroglyphs (ancient rock carvings) are visible at low tide. The beach is about 1 mile (2km) from the ferry terminal at the north end of town.

Dramatic 'shooters' are created as icebergs rush to the surface. Seals lounge on and around the icebergs.

The **Anan Bear and Wildlife Observatory**, 30 miles (48km) southeast of Wrangell (accessible by boat or plane), with a covered observation platform near cascading falls, affords a relatively safe and comfortable opportunity to observe black and brown bears during the peak salmon runs from late June to late August.

In the spring and fall, the **Stikine River** is visited by more than 120 species of migrating birds, including tundra swans, waterfowl, sandhill cranes, mergansers, and some 150,000 shore birds. In April, up to 1,600 eagles arrive to feed on the annual hooligan run, and thousands of snow geese pass through on their way north. Marine mammals in the area include whales, sea lions, and otters.

Chief Shakes Island, in the middle of Wrangell Harbor and accessed by walkway, is open to the public year round and offers close-up viewing of intricately carved Tlingit totems. The **Chief Shakes Tribal House** (open for cruise-ship arrivals or by appointment) is an example of ornate Tlingit architecture.

Petersburg

Traveling north along Wrangell Narrows, you'll discover 'Little Norway' on Mitkof Island – the town of **Petersburg**. The 3,100 residents of this quaint little Alaskan city are of Tlingit and Scandinavian descent. Peter Buschmann, a Norwegian immigrant, operated a cannery, sawmill and a dock in the area in 1900. His family's homestead grew into a community, and then a city by 1910.

Inaccessible by large cruise ships, Petersburg still has the feel of the small, bustling, fishing village it once was. It is known for its wide range of public art: murals, totems, sculpture, artistic sidewalk imprints, and Norwegian rosemaling (tole painting or decorative metalwork) on houses and storefronts. Petersburg's wildlife includes wolves, black bears, deer, goats, seals, whales, sea lions, and dolphins. More than 240 species of birds have been recorded on the island, including trumpeter swans. **Eagle Roost Park** offers a platform for viewing eagles roosting in trees, and a trail to the beach for additional birding or exploring tide pools.

Visitors can get a feel for Petersburg by strolling through the downtown area, and by

'Little Norway' – Petersburg

visiting the **Clausen Memorial Museum** (open Mon–Sat 10.30am–4.30pm; admission charge). The museum's gift shop stocks an interesting selection of local art and crafts.

During the summer, the historic **Sons of Norway Hall**, built in 1912, hosts a local buffet of Norwegian pastries, pickled herring and fish cakes (times vary depending on cruise-ship schedules). The event often includes local storytellers and a performance by the Leikerring Dance Group (local children wearing colorful Norwegian *bunad* national costumes). The **Bojer**

A humpback whale breaks the surface

Wikan Fisherman's Memorial Park, next door, is dedicated to those who have died at sea.

Local tour operators can arrange 'muskeg' walking tours, city tours, cannery tours, day cruises for **whale watching** at Frederick Sound, or trips to view nearby **LeConte Glacier** *(page 29)* by kayak, boat, plane, or helicopter. Visit the Petersburg Visitor Information Center (corner of First and Fram streets) for details or go to <www.petersburg.org>.

Sitka

Northwest of Petersburg, on the outer waters of the Inside Passage, is Baranof Island, and the beautiful seaside town of Sitka (population 8,800). First settled by Tlingits, invaded by Russian fur traders, then sold to the USA, today's Sitka shows the influence of a colorful history in a beautiful wilderness setting. The mild climate and rich habitat of the area makes it home to a wide variety of wildlife including brown bears and Sitka black-tailed deer. Tufted puffins, rhinoceros auklets, and other seabirds can be seen at **St Lazaria National Wildlife Refuge** (at the mouth of Sitka Sound). The waters surrounding Sitka are also home to sea otters, sea lions, and other marine life – including (in late fall and early spring) humpback whales. **Whale Park** (about 6 miles/10km south of downtown) features a boardwalk for whale viewing.

The Alaska Raptor Center (open mid-May–mid-Sept daily 8am–4pm; call to confirm weekend and winter hours; admission charge), with its goal of releasing rehabilitated birds to the wild, is a highlight for most visitors.

The **Harrigan Centennial Hall** provides visitor information, schedules, and locations for Russian, Ukranian and Tlingit dance performances, art, and wildlife displays. It is also the location of the **Isabel Miller Museum** (open May–Sept daily 8am–5pm; winter Tues–Sat 10am–4pm; donations welcome). The **Sheldon Jackson Museum** (104 College Drive; open mid-May–mid-Sept daily 9am–5pm; winter Tues–Sat 10am–4pm; admission charge) houses one of the state's largest and oldest collections of Native cultural artifacts.

The **Southeast Alaska Indian Cultural Center** (in **Sitka National Historical Park**; open May–Sept daily 8am–5pm; admission charge) offers a chance to see totem poles and to interact with local native artists.

Be sure to visit **Saint Michael's Cathedral** (open May–Sept Mon–Sat 9am–4pm, depending on cruise-ship visits, Sun by appointment; donation requested) to view Russian Orthodox art and church treasures.

Information on the various tours by bicycle, bus, boat, kayak, floatplane, and amphibious plane is available at the Harrigan Centennial Hall, the Sitka Convention and Visitors Bureau at 303 Lincoln Street, and at <www.sitka.org>.

Juneau

The state capital, **Juneau**, is located on Gastineau Channel (opposite Douglas Island), 900 miles (1,448km) northwest of Seattle, and 577 miles (925km) southeast of Anchorage, by air. Once a Tlingit fish camp, the area was flooded with prospectors after miners Joe Juneau and Richard Harris discovered gold in Gold Creek in 1880. Juneau became a city in 1900, and the territorial capital in 1906.

Today, Juneau has a slightly metropolitan feel – Alaska style. Nearly 45 percent of the 31,000 local residents are government employees, and the city has a thriving music, art, and theatre community. Downtown Juneau, with steep, narrow streets, gift shops, and art galleries, hunkers in the shadow of Mount Roberts. The Tongass National Forest setting and the rich Native culture, mining, fishing, and logging lend a distinctively Alaskan flair to this unique capital city.

Bowls, Alaska State Museum

The main **Visitor Center** for Juneau is located in the cruise-ship terminal. Visitor assistance and brochures are also available at the **Davis Log Cabin** (134 Third Street), the **US Forest Service** (in **Centennial Hall**, downtown), and at the **Marine Park Kiosk** (summer only) on the waterfront.

A stroll through the historic district of downtown Juneau includes the **Alaska State Museum** (open mid-May–mid-Sept daily 8.30am–

View of downtown Juneau

5.30pm; mid-Sept–mid-May Tues–Sat 10–4pm; admission charge); the **Native Cultural Museum** (in the Federal Building; open Mon–Fri 8.30am–4.30pm; free); the **Governor's House**; **Saint Nicholas Orthodox Church**; the **Juneau-Douglas City Museum** (open mid-May–Sept Mon–Fri 9am–5pm; Sat–Sun 10am–5pm; winter Tues–Sat noon–4pm; admission charge); and the **Last Chance Mining Museum** (open May–Sept daily 9.30am–12.30pm and 3.30pm–6.30pm; admission charge), at the end of Basin Road, above downtown.

If you are in Juneau on a clear day, take a trip up the **Mount Roberts Tramway** (open May 8–Sept 27 Sat–Sun 9am–9pm, Mon 10.30am–9pm, Tues–Fri 8am–9pm; May and Sept hours vary; admission charge). Board a tram car at the cruise-ship dock and travel to the 1,800-ft (548-m) level of the mountain for a panoramic view, Native art demonstrations, hiking trails, theater presentations, a restaurant, gift shop, and eagle exhibit.

Just south of town, **A J Mine/Gastineau Mill Enterprises** offers underground tours (daily; admission charge) that include a mining demonstration and an opportunity to pan for gold. Learn about fish hatcheries, watch salmon swim up a fish ladder, and see aquarium displays at the **Macaulay Salmon Hatchery** (2697 Channel Drive; open May–Sept Mon–Fri 10am–6pm, Sat–Sun 10am–5pm; admission charge).

Juneau's wildlife includes bald eagles, black bears, porpoises, sea lions, harbor seals, sea otters, mountain goats, and Sitka black-tailed deer. A unique chance for **observing brown bears** involves a short flight to a bear sanctuary at **Pack Creek**, in Kootznoowoo

The Wilderness Area of Admiralty Island can be accessed by boat or kayak, but it is a long and difficult journey. The USDA Forest Service issues a permits to the viewing areas every day, from June 1 to September 10, but prime viewing coincides with salmon runs, usually in July and August (tel: 907-586-8751 for permit information). Taking a **whale-watching** tour out of Juneau is an excellent way to see humpback and Orca (killer) whales, as well as other marine life and seabirds.

Glacier tours are another highlight of a visit to Juneau. **Mendenhall Glacier**, a part of the **Juneau Icefield** (and a top attraction), is a 13-mile (21-km) drive from downtown. The

---

Glacier Bay National Park and Preserve

The over 3.3 million acres (1.3 million hectares) of remote beaches, protected coves, tidewater glaciers, deep fjords, freshwater lakes, and towering mountains (some over 15,000ft/4,570m) make up the Glacier Bay National Park and Preserve. Accessible from Juneau by plane or boat, the park and preserve is the largest internationally protected area in the world. It is home to black and brown bears, moose, mountain goats, seals, and a vast array of bird species (including eagles). Recreational opportunities include boating, camping, kayaking, rafting, and mountaineering. More information is available at <www.nps.gov/glba>.

Iceberg, Mendenhall Glacier Lake

USDA Forest Service operates a visitor center there, and a variety of local tours – by plane, helicopter, or dog sled – will take you onto the ice. Day tours by boat, seaplane, or kayak of nearby twin **Sawyer Glaciers** in Tracy Arm, or of **Glacier Bay National Park and Preserve** *(see box opposite)* are available.

Gustavus

Forty-eight air miles (77km) northwest of Juneau, on the northern shore of Icy Passage, is the agricultural community of **Gustavus** (gus-*tay*-vuhs). Most of the 430 year-round residents enjoy a subsistence lifestyle with abundant natural resources, a mild climate, and spectacular scenery. Some 60,000 tourists travel through this community each year to see the 16 tidewater glaciers in the Glacier Bay National Park and Preserve. Gustavus can be reached by a 13-minute flight, or a scenic three-hour water-taxi trip from Juneau. Guests may stay in private lodges or inns within the community, or in the park at Glacier

Bay Lodge. The **Glacier Bay Visitor Center** (open May 27–Sept 11 daily; exhibits open 24 hours, desk noon–8.45pm) is located on the second floor of the lodge. The **Visitor Information Station** (open May and Sept 8am–5pm; June–Aug 7am–9pm) near the public-use dock in Bartlett Cove, offers permits, information, maps, and nautical charts for campers and recreational boaters in the park.

In addition to day cruises for glacier-viewing, activities include boating, camping, whale watching, mountain biking, golfing, and sea kayaking. In order to protect the local humpback whale population, the National Park Service limits the number of boats entering Glacier Bay by requiring permits between June 1 and August 31 (contact National Park Service at tel: 907-697-2268, or <www.nps.gov/glba>).

Haines

Haines (pop. 1,560) is set on the western shore of Lynn Canal, 80 air miles (128km) north of Juneau and 775 miles (1,247km) by road from Anchorage. The town was a mining supply center for Klondike gold prospectors in the 1890s, and the location of four canneries by the turn of the century. In 1904,

Bald eagle in the Chilkat Valley

Fort William H. Seward was built south of Haines. The area is home to two Indian villages: the Chilkoot, in Haines, and the Chilkat in nearby Klukwan.

Fort Seward has been restored and designated a national historic site. There are several interesting exhibits, including **Alaska Indian Arts** (open Mon–Fri 9am–5pm), which gives visitors a

Chilkat dancer, Haines

chance to watch local artists and carvers at work; and **Totem Village Tribal House** with scheduled performances (in summer) of **Chilkat Dancers' Storytelling Theater** (Mon–Fri pm; admission charge). In the **Sheldon Museum and Cultural Center** (open mid-May–mid-Sept Mon–Fri 11am–5pm, Sat– Sun 2–5pm; winter Mon–Fri 1–4pm; admission charge) exhibits illustrate the Tlingit, pioneer and military history of Haines. A favorite site for birders (and others) is the **Chilkat Bald Eagle Preserve** where (from October to January) you can see the world's largest congregation of bald eagles. Turnouts for eagle viewing and an information kiosk are located between Miles 18 and 21 of the Haines Highway. Haines celebrates the **Bald Eagle Festival** (see <www.baldeaglefest.org>) in the second week of November each year.

Tours of nearby attractions by bus, antique car, plane, boat, kayak, river raft, canoe, jet boat, and more can be arranged at the **Haines Convention and Visitors Center** *(see page 123).*

Skagway

At the northern end of Lynn Canal, in a narrow valley between two mountains, lies the picturesque town of **Skagway** (population 870). The name comes from the Tlingit 'Skagua,' or 'the place where the north wind blows.' In July 1897, gold was discovered in Canada's Klondike region, and the first boatload of prospectors arrived in Skagway. Access to Lake Bennett (where miners would build boats to float 500 miles/800km down the Yukon River to Dawson City) was either by the treacherous 33-mile (53-km) Chilkoot Trail (in nearby Dyea), or the perilous 40-mile (64-km) White Pass trail from Skagway. By October 1897, Skagway had become a bustling town with stores, saloons, gambling and dance houses, and some 20,000 residents. The **White Pass & Yukon Route Railroad** (daily departures May 10–Sept 24; admission charge), the first in Alaska, was built in 1898. The commerce it brought prevented Skagway from becoming a ghost town at the end of the gold rush in 1900. Skagway was linked to the Alaska Highway by the construction of the Klondike Highway in 1979.

Skagway is predominantly a tourist community. The White Pass & Yukon Route Railroad stopped year-round operations in 1982, and is now purely a tourist attraction. Skagway's downtown buildings have been colorfully restored to reflect the gold-rush days. The **Klondike Gold Rush National Historical Park** (open May–Sept daily 8am–6pm; winter Mon–Fri 8am–5pm; free) is Alaska's most-visited national park.

The sites in and around Skagway can be seen on foot or horseback, or by helicopter, plane, kayak, or raft. Local helicopter and dog-sled tours of the Denver Glacier (north of Skagway) are also available. For more information, visit the Skagway Convention and Visitors Bureau (*see page 124*) or <www.skagway.com>.

Yakutat

The 680 residents of **Yakutat** (*Yack*-uh-tat) live in an isolated area along the rugged northern coast of the Gulf of Alaska, surrounded by the **Wrangell-St Elias National Park, Malaspina Glacier** and **Tongass National Forest**. The **Hubbard Glacier**, 30 miles (48km) north at the mouth of Russell Fjord, is determining the future of Yakutat by its recent dramatic movements. In 2002, the glacier blocked the fjord for the second time since 1986, creating a huge lake. Fortunately, the dam again gave way, avoiding terrible flooding.

Explorers and fur traders first encountered Yakutat's Tlingit Natives in the 18th and 19th centuries. In 1903, a cannery, sawmill, store, and railroad were built, and the cannery operated through to 1970.

Contemporary goldpanner

Yakutat's economy is now based on fishing, fish processing, and government. Most residents live a subsistence lifestyle of hunting and fishing. The area receives some of the heaviest rainfall in the state. The mild, maritime climate is compatible with a variety of wildlife, including brown bears, mountain goats, wolves, moose, sea lions, whales, bald eagles, swans, falcons, and seabirds.

Yakutat can be accessed by regular scheduled commercial flights, and by the Alaska Marine Highway Ferry in spring, summer and early fall.

SOUTHCENTRAL ALASKA

Traveling 650 miles (1,045km) north of the lush rainforests of Southeast Alaska to the drier, open country of Southcentral, feels like coming up from underground. In Southcentral, you orient yourself by looking at the distant horizon: the Alaska Range to the north, the Chugach and St Elias Mountains to the east, the Aleutian Range to the west, and the Gulf of Alaska to the south. Most Southcentral communities get far less rainfall (Anchorage averages 16ins/40cm per year) than those on the Panhandle. Notable exceptions are the communities of Prince William Sound, which enjoy a maritime climate (similar to Southeast, but with colder win-

Anchorage, Alaska's largest city

ters). The Gulf of Alaska, warmed by the Japanese current, moderates summer and winter temperatures in Southcentral. Nearly two-thirds of all Alaskans call this area home.

Anchorage

Anchorage began as a tent city in 1915, a construction camp for workers building the 470-mile (756-km) **Alaska Railroad** from Seward to Fairbanks. With the railroad as its economic base, the town grew from a tent city on Ship Creek to become an incorporated city in 1920. Today, 277,000 Anchorage residents make up nearly half of the total population of Alaska.

Begin your exploration of Anchorage at the sod-roofed **Log Cabin Visitor Information Center** (corner of Fourth Ave and F Street; open June–Aug daily 7.30am–7pm; May and Sept 8am–6pm; Oct–Apr 9am–4pm). A walking tour map, an *Anchorage Visitor's Guide* and the Alaska Department of Fish and Game's *Anchorage Wildlife Viewing Hotspots* are among the helpful publications available there.

It would be well worth your time to walk across the street to the **Alaska Public Lands Information Center** (open mid-May–mid-Sept daily 9am–5pm; winter Mon–Fri 10am–5pm) to view wildlife and cultural exhibits and interactive videos. The informative staff will be happy to answer questions regarding Alaska's public lands use. Then head over to the

Town Square Municipal Park, on Fifth Avenue, sit down on a bench among the flowers, look through the brochures, and plan your visit to Alaska's largest city. You may be treated to a public concert.

One of the more remarkable options – on the waterside of downtown Anchorage – is the chance to join local people for salmon fishing (state license required) or just to observe huge kings and silvers swimming upstream to spawn at **Ship Creek**. Don't miss the **Museum of History and Art** (corner of 7th Ave and A Street; open mid-May–mid-Sept daily 9am–6pm; winter Wed–Sat 10am–6pm, Sun noon–5pm; admission charge), where you can catch up on 10,000 years of Alaska's history and culture. The gift shop features books on local history as well as Native art, crafts and jewelry. The **Oscar Anderson House Museum** (420 M Street at Elderberry Park; open June–Sept for guided tours; admission charge) is one of the earliest pioneer houses in Anchorage. Visitors of all ages will enjoy a trip to the **Imaginarium Science Discovery Center** (737 West Fifth Ave; open Mon–Sat 10am–6pm, Sun noon–5pm; admission charge) for hands-on exploration, including marine tanks, a planetarium, the aurora borealis, reptiles, and a bubble lab.

Exterior of the Museum of History and Art, Anchorage

Another chance for interactive learning is found at the **Alaska Experience Theater & Alaska Earthquake Exhibit** (705 W Sixth Ave), where you will feel the earth move as you watch a 180-degree, three dimensional screen presentation of Alaska's history, including the 9.2 magnitude earthquake of 1964, the largest to hit North America.

At the Fur Rendezvous, held in Anchorage each February, popular attractions include snow sculpting, zany games of snowshoe softball, and sled-dog races. Dancing salmon and skiing penguins are among the figures sculpted out of snow. The finished creations draw hundreds of people to the display site north of downtown.

If you head to East Anchorage (toward the mountains) you can visit the **Alaska Native Heritage Center** (off Muldoon Road; open May–Sept daily 9am–6pm; winter Sat 10am–5pm; admission charge; courtesy buses available from downtown locations) where you will meet Alaska's first people through interactive Native art, storytelling, dance, and song. While you're on the east side of town, drop by the **Alaska Botanical Gardens** (4601 Campbell Airstrip Road; open mid-May–mid-Sept daily 9am–9pm; winter during daylight hours; admission charge). Stroll through 110 acres (45 hectares) of spruce and birch woodlands, enjoy a variety of gardens, and learn about the native flora of Southcentral Alaska

Twenty minutes northeast of downtown Anchorage on the Glenn Highway is the access road to **Arctic Valley**, a ski resort in winter, and a scenic hiking, mountain biking, and berry picking hot spot in summer. A bit farther northeast on 'the Glenn' will take you to the community of Eagle River and the **Eagle River Nature Center** (mile 12.5 Eagle River Road; open June–Aug daily Mon–Thur 10am–5pm, Fri–Sat 10am–7pm; May and Sept Tues–Sun 10am–5pm; winter Fri–Sun

10am–5pm; free admission; parking fee), with hiking trails, a viewing telescope, natural history displays, and nature programs. Continue northeast for another 13 miles (20km), and you will come to the Athabascan village of **Eklutna** (population 371) and **Eklutna National Historic Park** (Eklutna exit, turn left; open mid-May–mid-Sept daily; admission charge). This small park features a museum, gift shop, the historic Saint Nicholas Russian Orthodox Church, and a cemetery with colorful spirit houses.

A number of attractions are located in South Anchorage. The **Alaska Zoo** (4731 O'Malley Road; open daily 9am–6pm, Tues and Fri until 9pm; admission charge) offers viewing of nearly 100 birds and mammals in a woodland setting. The kids will enjoy a trip to **H2Oasis** (1520 O'Malley Road; open June–Aug daily 10am–10pm; winter Mon–Fri 3–9pm, Sat–Sun 10am–9pm; admission charge), Alaska's only indoor water park. South of Anchorage, the Seward Highway, a National Scenic Byway, travels along the northern shore of Turnagain Arm through Chugach State Park and Chugach National Forest.

Just beyond the residential area is the **Anchorage Coastal Wildlife Refuge (Potter Marsh)**, which provides excellent habitat for a variety of resident and migratory birds. A wooden boardwalk winds through the marsh and over Rabbit Creek, where spawning salmon may be seen. The historic **Potter Section House**, just south of Potter Marsh, was once housing for railroad maintenance workers. Now it is the **Chugach State Park Headquarters**, a source of brochures, maps, and information on the park. **Beluga Point**, about 5 miles (8km) farther south, is a rocky neck of land that juts into Turnagain Arm – a prime spot to sight beluga whales from mid-July through August. A few additional miles south will take you to **Windy Corner**, a bend in the road where Dall sheep can often be seen along the side of the road.

Landing on Lake Hood

West Anchorage offers excellent birding opportunities on **Lake Hood** and **Lake Spenard**, near the Ted Stevens International Airport. Flocks of local and migratory birds share these lakes with fleets of local and migratory seaplanes. The **Alaska Aviation Heritage Museum** (on Lake Hood, 4721 Aircraft Drive; open mid-May–mid-Sept daily 9am–5pm; winter Fri–Sun 10am–4pm; admission charge) is a good place to learn about Alaska's aviation history and view vintage aircraft. On the other side of the airport **Kincaid Park** offers a variety of woodland hiking trails and scenic views, and is home to many of Anchorage's resident moose.

One of the best ways to experience Anchorage is to cycle, walk, or ski the 120 miles (194km) of award-winning trails that criss-cross it. The 11-mile (17-km) **Tony Knowles Coastal Trail** begins downtown and follows the coast to Kincaid Park (be alert for moose). A map of Anchorage trails is available at the Alaska Public Lands Information Office *(see page 122)*.

The Matanuska-Susitna Valley

In 1934, during the Great Depression, the government invited farmers from the poverty-stricken mid-western states to come to Alaska and establish agricultural colonies. The headquarters of the project, known as the Matanuska Valley Experiment, was in the town of Palmer. Colonists, 203 families in all, were promised free transportation to Alaska, housing, and 40-acre (16-hectare) tracts of farmland for as little as $5 per acre. Upon arrival, they struggled with fickle weather, variable soil conditions, and measles and scarlet fever. Discouraged, many of them left; by 1948, only 40 original pioneer families remained.

Much of the farmland (now the Matanuska-Susitna Valley) has become residential – suburbs for Anchorage commuters. The remaining farmers and backyard gardeners in 'the Valley' benefit from Alaska's long summer days and lack of pests and grow a variety of hardy, sometimes giant, produce.

Prize specimens in the Matanuska Valley

Palmer

Today, **Palmer** (population 5,200) still feels like a small-town farming community. The **Visitor Center** shares a building with the **Chamber of Commerce** and the **Palmer Museum** (723 S. Valley Road; open May–mid-Sept daily 9am–6pm; winter Mon–Fri 10am–4pm; donations welcome).

> If you are in Palmer in late August or early September, don't miss the Alaska State Fair, where you can check out the Giant Vegetable Exhibit. Local residents compete to see who can grow the largest vegetables. The record cabbage weighed 105.6lb (48kg).

The museum exhibits colony-era household relics as well as farming and woodworking tools, a gift shop and garden. At the **Colony House Museum** (316 E. Elmwood Ave; open May–Aug Mon–Sat noon–4pm; admission charge), a refurbished 1935 farmhouse, you'll hear stories about Palmer's early days told by a direct descendent of the original pioneer families.

One of the most beautiful areas of Palmer is Hatcher Pass, the site of **Independence Mine Historical State Park** (visitor center open mid-June–early Sept daily 10am–7pm, depending on road conditions; parking and guided tour fees). It is listed on the National Register of Historic Places and details the area's gold-mining history. Take a tour through restored mining buildings, or try panning for gold. In winter, Hatcher Pass is a popular sporting area, for alpine skiing, snowboarding, and snowmachining (in designated areas).

The **Musk Ox Farm** (Mile 50, Glenn Highway; open early May–Sept daily 10am–6pm; winter by appointment; admission charge) offers a rare chance to see one of the Arctic's oldest living species, and to learn of the interesting project that supplies *qiviut* (the soft under-wool of the musk ox) to Oomingmak, an Alaskan Native knitters' cooperative.

Wasilla

Originally a supply base for the region's gold and coal mining operations, the town site of **Wasilla** was established in 1917. Today, the city has a population of about 6,100, an estimated 30 percent of whom commute daily to jobs in Anchorage.

In the center of town, the **Dorothy Page Museum** (323 W. Main Street; open June–Aug Tues–Sat 9am–5pm; winter Mon–Fri 9am–5pm; admission charge) is the site of the first schoolhouse in the area, and offers exhibits on the history of mining, homesteading, dog mushing, and the Iditarod Trail. The **Museum of Alaska Transportation and Industry** (Mile 47 Parks Highway; open May–Sept Tues–Sun 10am–5pm; winter Sat 10am–5pm; admission charge) features the boats, planes, fire trucks, trains (and more) of Alaska's past, plus antique agricultural and mining equipment.

Wasilla is home to the annual re-start of the Iditarod Sled Dog Race. Visit the **Iditarod Trail Sled Dog Race Headquarters** (Mile 2.2 Knik-Goose Bay Road; open mid-May–mid-Sept daily 8am–7pm; winter Mon–Fri 8am–5pm) for information about the official state sport of Alaska, a gift shop, and a chance to take a short dog sled ride. To learn more about the race, and about the community of Knik, continue a few miles down the same road to the **Knik Museum** (Mile 13.9 Knik-Goose Bay Road; open June–mid-Sept daily noon–6pm; admission charge) and the **Mushers' Hall of Fame**.

Iditarod

Alaskans love the Iditarod, a 1,100-mile (1,770-km) sled dog race that starts (ceremonially) in Anchorage the first Saturday of every March, restarts (for real) in Wasilla, and then high-tails it all the way across the state to Nome. The 2005 winner of the race, Robert Sorlie (of Norway), made the trip in 9 days, 18 hours and 40 minutes.

Talkeetna

Talkeetna (population 844), a mining town and trading post in 1896, still reflects its rustic, frontier past. The town's proximity to Mount McKinley makes it a staging area for mountain climbers. It's an ideal place to view the mountain, and a number of tour companies in town offer opportunities for flight-seeing, jet-boat trips, fishing, and river rafting.

A walking tour through Talkeetna's downtown area (listed on the National Register of Historic Places) reveals two blocks of interesting log cabins and clapboard buildings, reflecting the gold-rush days of the past. The **Talkeetna Historical Society Museum** (open year-round on a varying schedule; admission charge) consists of six buildings, including a one-room schoolhouse and a trapper's cabin.

Fishing in the Talkeetna River

Denali State Park, not to be confused with Denali National Park and Preserve, is located at the northern edge of the Matanuska-Susitna Borough near Trapper Creek. The park provides opportunities for camping, rafting, canoeing, flightseeing, hiking, and views of McKinley.

Girdwood

About 35 miles (56km) south of Anchorage, as the Seward Highway winds along Turnagain Arm, you'll find **Girdwood**, where the **Alyeska Ski Resort** draws skiers and snowboarders from Southcentral and beyond in winter. Year round, an aerial tram ride takes tourists to an observation deck and restaurant at the 2,300-ft (700-m) level of Mount Alyeska.

The richest gold mine in Southcentral, **Crow Creek Mine** (3 miles/5km from Alyeska Resort on Crow Creek Road; open May 15–Oct 1 daily 9am–6pm; admission charge) is a popular recreational mining site for visitors and local people. Dress warmly, bring rain gear, mosquito repellent, food, and a camera. Experienced hikers, armed with adequate hiking gear and supplies, may enjoy the spectacular **Crow Pass Trail.**

Portage

For guaranteed wildlife viewing, stop at the **Alaska Wildlife Conservation Center** (open mid-May–mid-Sept 8am–8pm; winter 10am–5pm; admission charge). The 120-acre (48-ha), drive-through refuge cares for a wide variety of orphaned, injured or sick animals, unable to survive in the wild.

Portage Glacier and the **Begich Boggs Visitor Center** (open late May–early Sept daily 9am–6pm; winter Sat–Sun 10am–4pm) is Alaska's most popular visitor attraction. Forest Service interpreters are on hand to answer questions about the area's historical and natural wonders. A film, *Voices from the Ice*, is shown hourly during the summer (admission charge).

Continuing on the Portage Glacier Highway, you'll soon arrive at the 2½-mile (4-km) long, single-lane **Anton Anderson Memorial Tunnel** (open summer daily 5.30am–11.55pm; winter 8.30am–5:45pm; vehicles may travel, in alternating directions, at 15-minute intervals; toll charged).

Prince William Sound

Next stop is Whittier, at the head of Passage Canal, a fjord of **Prince William Sound**. This huge body of water, rimmed by mountains and glaciers, cut by fjords, and teeming with wildlife, is one of Alaska's great natural wonders.

Whittier

Whittier (population 172), surrounded by towering mountains and the largest concentration of glaciers in Alaska, enjoys one of the state's most stunning backdrops. The area's protected water is excellent for kayak adventures and allows comfortable day-cruises for viewing glaciers and marine life (including otters, porpoises and whales). The town itself, though decidedly less picturesque, is certainly unusual. Nearly all of the residents live in a single, 14-story, concrete building, originally built in 1940 as army housing. The building also houses the town's medical clinic and grocery store.

Whittier experiences significant amounts of rainfall in summer, snowfall in winter and year-round windy conditions. You should dress warmly, in layers, even in summer, and bring a camera.

Glacier in Prince William Sound

Valdez

The earliest settlers of the town of **Valdez** (pronounced Val-*deez*) were duped into coming here. In the winter of 1897–98, promising tales of an established trail to the gold fields of Interior Alaska, the 'All American Trail,' brought 4,000 would-be miners to the area. They arrived, however, to a daunting discovery: no town, and no real trail. A tent city sprang up, and as gold and copper mining flourished in the area, so did the town. Today Valdez has a population of about 3,750.

It first made international news following the devastating 1964 Alaska earthquake, when 31 residents died in the resulting tsunami, and the rest were forced to move what was left of their town to higher ground. In 1973, the US Congress approved plans for the Trans-Alaska Oil Pipeline, with its southern terminus in Valdez. In 1989, the oil tanker *Exxon Valdez* ran aground on Bligh Reef in Prince William Sound, causing the largest oil spill in North American history.

Valdez is also famous for heavy snowfall, averaging 325ins (82cm) a year in the city, and 552ins (140cm) a year in nearby Thompson Pass. Winter-sports enthusiasts, from the sedate to the extreme, come here to enjoy skiing, snowboarding, snowmachining, dog sledding, and ice climbing.

Favorite summer activities include fishing, rafting, and kayaking, or rock climbing in the spectacular **Keystone Canyon** (with its towering falls). Valdez has several excellent hiking trails for all experience levels (beware of bears), one of which parallels Mineral Creek and leads to the **Stamp Mill** (left over Gold Rush days).

Valdez offers birding, wildlife viewing, glacier cruising, and flightseeing throughout the summer and fall. Or you can take a leisurely stroll through local history exhibits at the **Valdez Museum** (217 Egan Drive; open mid-May–mid-Sept daily 9am–6pm; winter Mon–Fri 1–5pm, Sat noon–4pm; admission charge). Stop by the **Visitor Information Center** (200

Fairbanks Drive; open mid-May–mid-Sept daily 8am–8pm; <www.valdezalaska.org> for details).

Access to Valdez is via regularly scheduled air service from Anchorage, the Alaska Marine Highway ferry system or by driving the Richardson Highway.

Cordova

Cordova lies at the southeastern end of Prince William Sound. It was originally inhabited by Alutiiq people, but migrating Athabascans and Tlingits (called Eyaks) have also lived in the area – and still do. Just after the turn of the 20th century, Cordova

Sea lions near Valdez

became an important shipping hub for iron ore mined in the Kennecott Mine, and shipped to the coast via the Copper River and Northwestern Railroad. In the early 1940s, commercial fishing became the community's economic base, as copper production decreased and the railroad was abandoned. Today the 2,300 residents of this attractive seaport still rely on commercial fishing and a subsistence lifestyle. Somewhat off the beaten path of tourist destinations, Cordova is not for everyone, and local people say that's okay with them.

One of the main highlights is in early May, when more than 5 million shore birds pause, during their annual migration, to rest and feed in the tidal flats of the **Copper River Delta**. The **Copper River Delta Shorebird Festival** draws bird lovers from all over the world. Other summer activities include fishing for the famed Wild Copper River Salmon, and exploring the local sights by canoe, raft, bike, or on foot.

The **Cordova Historical Museum** (Centennial Building, First Street; open Mon–Fri 10am–6pm, Sat 1–5pm, Sun noon–3pm; donations welcome) features historical information on the Copper River, Bering River, and Prince William Sound. If you'd like a rare chance to see an orca (killer whale) skeleton, go to the **Ilanka Cultural Center and Museum** (110 Nicholoff Street; open Mon–Fri 10am–5pm or by appointment; donations welcome). Sponsored by the Native Village of Eyak, the center displays Native artifacts and artwork, and offers art classes (in summer) and a gift gallery.

Cordova is accessible by regular air service from Anchorage, and by the Alaska Marine Highway System.

The Kenai Peninsula

The first people of the Kenai Peninsula were the Kenaitze Indians. It is an area rich in natural resources, often considered to be the playground of Southcentral Alaska. The Captain Cook State Recreation Area, Chugach National Forest, Kenai National Wildlife Refuge, Kachemak Bay State Park, and Kenai Fjords National Park make 'the Kenai' a favorite recreational destination for hiking, camping, boating, biking, wildlife viewing, and especially fishing. During the summer, the Seward and Sterling highways are lined with cars, trucks and motor homes headed south, especially on three-day weekends, or when any type of salmon is running.

Seward

The city of **Seward** (population 2,500) is on the eastern side of the peninsula, by Resurrection Bay. Once the major port for Alaska, Seward is blessed with a gorgeous seaside setting, backed by steep mountains. One of those, **Mount Marathon**, draws runners from around the world to compete in a grueling race to the 3022-ft (921-m) peak (and back) every July 4th.

Don't miss the **Alaska SeaLife Center** (301 Railway Ave; open mid-April–mid-Sept daily 8am–7pm; winter 10am–5pm; admission charge), where huge tanks with under-water viewing windows allow close observation of local marine wildlife.

Kenai Fjords National Park and Soldotna

Take a day cruise into the incredible **Kenai Fjords National Park**. Aside from excellent glacier viewing, you'll see exotic seabirds and, just maybe, stellar sea lions, harbor seals, Dall's porpoises, sea otters, and humpback, killer, or minke whales. Remember to dress in warm layers, even in summer.

There are many other interesting sights in the area, including **Exit Glacier** (Herman Leirer Road, Mile 3 Seward

Seward is the northern terminus for most cruise ships crossing the Gulf of Alaska

Taking in the views at Kenai

Highway; open year round; admission fee May–Sept; no road maintenance in winter) and the **Exit Glacier Nature Center** (open late May–early Sept 9am–8.30pm; admission charge). For additional information on the area, go to the **Visitor Center** (on 4th Avenue at the small boat harbor).

Seward is accessible by car, bus, Alaska Marine Highway ferry, and the Alaska Railroad. Drop by the **Seward Visitor Center** (on the right as you come into town) for additional information, or go to <www.seward.com>.

On the western side of the peninsula is the city of **Soldotna** (population 3,800), the central hub of the Kenai. It is the main shopping district, and a great jumping-off point for the various recreational opportunities in the area. The **Russian River** is a hot spot for sport fishing. When the salmon are running, you'll see hipwader-clad fishermen along the shores, shoulder to shoulder, casting and reeling in a roughly synchronized cadence ('combat fishing').

You can learn about recreational activities and wildlife viewing in the 2-million acre (81,000-ha) **Kenai National Wildlife Refuge** at the visitor center 1 mile (2km) south of Soldotna, on Ski Hill Road (open June–Aug Mon–Fri 8am–4.30pm, Sat–Sun 9am–5pm; winter Mon–Fri 8am–4.30pm, Sat–Sun 10am–5pm). The **Soldotna Homestead Museum** (44790 Sterling Highway; open mid-May–mid-Sept Tues–Sat 10am–4pm, Sun noon–4pm; donations welcome) features wildlife displays and Native artifacts in an authentic homesteaders' village.

A short distance up the Kenai Spur Highway from Soldotna is the city of **Kenai** (population 6,800). Kenai was incorporated in 1960, three years after an oil discovery on the Swanson River. The city has excellent views of Cook Inlet, four active volcanoes, two mountain ranges, and the Kenai River. In mid-April, the tidal marshes of the **Kenai River Flats** (take the Bridge Access Road to Kalifornsky Beach Road) offers birders a chance to see up to 5,000 snow geese (a day) en route to nesting grounds in Siberia. Numerous other waterfowl and waterbirds can be seen at the Flats, and from mid-May to early June the area is a calving ground for caribou. Other wildlife sighting possibilities include eagles and, near the river mouth, beluga whale and harbor seals.

Check out the **Kenai Visitors' and Cultural Center** (11471 Kenai Spur Highway; open mid-May–mid-Sept Mon–Fri 9am–8pm, Sat–Sun 11am–7pm; winter Mon–Fri 9am–5pm,

Scenery along the Seward Highway on the Kenai Peninsula

Sat 11am–4pm; admission charge), which offers a summer art show and permanent exhibits on Native and Russian culture, as well as homesteading, mining, commercial fishing, and oil industry history displays. The facility has a natural history room featuring birds, fish, and mammals. Maps for a walking tour of the historic Old Town are available as well.

Homer

At the southern tip of the Kenai Peninsula is the artsy hamlet of **Homer** (population 5,300) on Kachemak Bay. In the downtown area are small art galleries, gift shops, and restaurants. The Homer Spit, a narrow finger of land jutting out into the bay, is a popular spot for visitors to eat, shop for souvenirs, arrange for tours, or buy fresh seafood.

➤   The **Alaska Islands & Ocean Visitor Center** (95 Sterling Highway; open late May–early Sept daily 9am–6pm; winter

Fishing out of Homer

Tues–Sat 10am–5pm; free) is an interpretive, educational, and research facility, dedicated to the understanding and conservation of the marine environment. You can learn about the natural and cultural history of the Kenai, and see art exhibits, a homestead cabin, a nature trail, and botanical garden at the **Pratt Museum** (3779 Bartlett Street; open mid-May–mid-Sept daily 10am–6pm; winter Tues–Sun noon–5pm; admission charge). Go to the **Homer Visitor and Information Center** (201 Sterling Highway; open mid-May–mid-Sept daily 9am–5pm; winter Mon–Fri 9am–5pm; <www.homer-alaska.org>) for information on fishing, sightseeing, flightseeing, whale watching, bear viewing, and birding in Homer, and in the communities of **Halibut Cove** and **Seldovia** (a short trip across the bay by ferry, water taxi, or airplane).

Kodiak

Kodiak Island is one of a chain in the Gulf of Alaska known as the Kodiak Archipelago. Sometimes called Alaska's Emerald Isle, Kodiak is carpeted with lush vegetation, due to the area's mild, maritime climate. It has been home to the Native Alutiiq people for over 7,500 years. Abundant sea-otter populations drew Russian fur traders to the area in the late 1700s, and eventually Kodiak became the first capital of Russian America. With the purchase of Alaska by the United States in 1867, Kodiak's economic base shifted to salmon. Today, Kodiak Island is home to the city of Kodiak (population 6,200), and to six Native villages (with populations ranging from 26 to 238) dotting the island's coastline: Akhiok, Karluk, Larsen Bay, Old Harbor, Ouzinkie and Port Lions. A US Coast Guard Station is located just south of the city.

The **Kodiak Visitor Information Center** (100 Marine Way; open mid-June–mid-Sept Mon–Fri 8am–5pm, Sat–Sun times vary due to ferry schedule; winter Mon–Fri 8am–noon, 1–5pm) is the place to begin your tour. The center has information and maps, including one for a walking tour of the city. Kodiak averages a 12-ft (3.6-m) tidal variation: consult a local tide book to see when the next minus tide is expected, then check out the creatures of the intertidal zone (anemones, sea stars, sunbursts, and more). Steller sea lions, sea otters, and fin, minke, humpback, killer, and gray whales swim in the waters. The island is a favorite site for birders – over 200 species have been identified locally. But Kodiak's most famous resident is the huge Kodiak brown bear, approximately 3,000 of which roam the archipelago while about 2,000 more live 30 miles (48km) across Shelikof Strait in the **Katmai National Park and Preserve**. The **Kodiak National Wildlife Refuge Visitor Center** (1390 Buskin River Road; open late May–Aug Mon– Fri 8am–7pm, Sat–Sun noon–4pm; winter Mon–Fri

---

Avoiding Close Encounters with Bears

Most visitors consider seeing a bear in the wilds of Alaska a highlight of their trip. But this is not Disneyland. Knowing a few facts about bear behavior may help keep you – and the bears – safe.

• Bears are curious, intelligent, and potentially dangerous.

• Most bears try to avoid people. Make your presence known through whistling, singing, talking loudly, or wearing bear bells. It may feel silly, but surprising a bear feels worse. Group travel is best. Avoid thick brush; bears can navigate it better than you.

• Don't camp on a trail. Bears (and moose) like to take the easy way, too. Avoid camping near areas scented by fish or animal carcasses.

• Use long lenses to photograph bears. Resist taking close-up shots.

• Feeding bears (intentionally or carelessly) is dangerous and illegal. Cook away from your tent and store food away from your campsite (hang it from trees, if possible, or use air-tight containers). Avoid strong-smelling foods such as bacon or smoked fish. Keep your camp clean, burn all garbage, and haul out any remains.

8am–4.30pm) has informa-
tion on plants, wildlife, and
recreational opportunities.
Cabins, campsites, picnic
areas, and hiking trails are
also available on public lands
managed by **Alaska State
Parks, Kodiak District**
(1400 Abercrombie Drive).
Whether you are in the city
or backcountry, remember
that Kodiak Island (like most
of Alaska) is bear country.

Brown bears in Katmai Park

Learn about Kodiak's first people at the **Alutiiq Museum
and Archaeological Repository** (215 Mission Road; open
June–Aug Mon–Fri 9am–5pm, Sat 10am–5pm, Sun by
appointment; winter Tues–Fri 9am–5pm, Sat 10.30am–
4.30pm; admission charge). You can view historic and pre-
historic objects from the Aleutian Islands and the Kodiak
Archipelago at the **Baranof Museum** (Erskine House, 101
Marine Way; open late May–early Sept Mon–Sat 10am–
4pm, Sun noon–4pm; winter Tues–Sat 10am–3pm; admission charge). The **Holy Resurrection Russian Orthodox
Church** (next to the Baranof Museum) reflects the lasting
influence of the Russian Orthodox religion, as does the
**Kodiak Museum of the History of the Orthodox Church
in Alaska** (414 Mission Road; open Mon–Fri 10am–4pm, or
by appointment; free). **Fort Abercrombie State Historical
Park**, an army outpost in World War II, offers various recreational opportunities, plus exhibits on Kodiak's military history. The Miller Point Gun Bunker houses the Kodiak
Military History Museum (open June–Aug Mon, Wed,
Sat–Sun 1–4pm; May and Sept Sat–Sun 1–4pm; winter by
appointment; admission charge).

Majestic Mount McKinley

INTERIOR ALASKA

Alaska's vast interior basin is a study in extremes. Bordered on the north by the Brooks Range and to the south by the Alaska Range, it is where you'll find some of the state's most spectacular natural wonders: Mount McKinley (in Denali National Park), the Yukon River (the longest in Alaska), hot springs, a wealth of wildlife, and breathless displays of the aurora borealis. The Interior is frigid in winter; temperatures plunge to –60°F (–50°C). What may surprise you is that summers can sizzle, reaching the upper 90sºF (around 36ºC). Daylight also varies greatly. Fairbanks has over 21 hours of sunlight at the summer solstice, but less than four hours at the winter solstice.

Denali National Park and Preserve

One of the primary incentives for visiting Alaska's Interior is to see the tallest mountain in North America, Mount McKinley (called Denali by Alaskans), within **Denali National Park and**

Preserve. This 20,320-ft (7,071-m) behemoth is among the many commanding peaks of the Alaska Range. The 6 million-acre (2.4 million-ha) park, established in 1917 then expanded and renamed in 1980, provides breath-taking scenery and thrilling wildlife (Dall sheep, moose, wolves, grizzly bears, and more). Other popular activities include mountaineering (advanced registration required), biking, and backcountry camping (permit required).

The entrance to the park is 240 miles (385km) north of Anchorage, and 125 miles (200km) south of Fairbanks on the George Parks Highway. The mountaineering headquarters is in Talkeetna, about 100 miles (160km) north of Anchorage. Denali is accessible from Anchorage or Fairbanks by car, bus, or van service, private plane, or the Alaska Railroad. There is a single road reaching 92 miles (148km) into the park. Private motorized traffic is allowed only as far as Savage River Check Station at Mile 15 of the Park Road, beyond which, in order to minimize impact on wildlife, the National Park Service only allows travel on foot, by bicycle, or by the bus service provided by the park concessionaire.

The visitor season at Denali National Park runs from early May to mid-September, depending on weather conditions. There are three free shuttle-bus options to points of interest within the entrance area of the park (schedules and pick-up sites are posted). One of the shuttles will take you to view a sled-dog demonstration, 2½ miles (4km) down the Roadside Trail (no private vehicle parking).

The Visitor Transportation System, or park shuttle, is designed to allow visitors to see remote areas of the park, or to access a campground or hiking trails. You may disembark along the route, then

In July 2004, Mario Locatelli, age 71 years 6 months, became the oldest person to reach the summit of Mount McKinley, the highest peak in North America.

> Alaska offers many opportunities to walk on glaciers, but this activity should be attempted only with an experienced guide, or with the advice of local experts, training, and the proper equipment.

reboard another shuttle on a space-available basis. Shuttle drivers will (informally) assist in spotting wildlife along the road and answer questions concerning the park. Rest stops are made at one-hour intervals (approximately). Bear in mind that food concessions are not available beyond the entrance area. Some, but not all, rest stops will have water. Bring sufficient food and water. Buses have very little storage space, and you will have to hold your food, jackets, cameras, backpacks, etc. The weather at Denali is variable: dress in layers and bring a light, hooded jacket, even in summer.

Also remember that children under 4 years and/or under 40 pounds (18kg) *must* be in a child safety seat, which you must provide. Wheelchair-accessible buses are available, but you must ask for one when you make reservations.

There is a basic park entrance fee. Additional shuttle charges depend on how far you travel. Advance reservations are recommended, and can be made online (<www.reservedenali.com>), by fax, phone, mail, or in person *(see page 118)*.

For more comfort you could take one of the two (more expensive) bus tours: the 5-hour Denali Natural History Tour, or the 8-hour (4-hour during shoulder seasons) Teklanika Tundra Wilderness Tour. Both tours provide formal, interpretive programs, a snack or box lunch, and hot drinks. Reservations by phone, fax, or in person *(see page 118)*.

For campers needing transportation to campgrounds or backcountry units within the park, there are special camper buses, which have room for backpacks and bikes, and will drop you off at any point along the park road, unless a particular area is closed or if wildlife is in the immediate vicinity.

Reservations for these buses are available at the Wilderness Access Center when you receive your backcountry permit.

Lodging is available outside the park along the highway, and in Healy or Talkeetna. The demand for rooms is fierce and reservations must be made well in advance. There are a few privately owned lodges (and one airstrip) within the park, each offering a variety of tour packages. Flightseeing tours may be arranged out of Anchorage, Talkeetna, and Fairbanks, or at the park entrance. Check the following websites: <www.nps.gov/dena>; <www.denalichamber.com>; <www.anchorage.net>; <www.explorefairbanks.com>.

Fairbanks

The city of Fairbanks, Alaska's 'Golden Heart' city, was founded by coincidence. In August of 1901, an entrepreneur called E.T. Barnette, along with his supplies, was put ashore on the

At home on the range, Interior Alaska

bank of the Chena River when a sternwheeler, en route to Tanacross, became stranded in shallow water. Barnette had planned to establish a trading post at the halfway point on the Valdez to Eagle trail used by prospectors headed for the Klondike. Coincidentally, two prospectors, in need of supplies, witnessed the off-loading of Barnette's cargo. Barnette sold the men the goods they needed to continue their search for gold. Several months later the miners, Felix Pedro and Tom Cleary, struck serious pay dirt. As word of the gold strike spread and other miners rushed to the area, Barnette decided to locate his trading post there on the banks of the Chena River, and Barnette's Cache, later known as Fairbanks, soon sprouted.

The Fairbanks Northstar Borough is the second-most populous area within Alaska. Its resourceful residents know how to brave (and enjoy) dark, bitterly cold winters (−60°F/ −50°C and below), while distracting themselves with winter sports (including championship sled-dog races), winter carnivals, fireworks and ice-sculpting competitions – frequently beneath dazzling displays of the aurora borealis (northern lights). During the summer, residents work and play hard

The Alaska Railroad

The Alaska Railroad is one of the last full-service railroads in the United States and provides passenger and freight operations for communities from Seward to Fairbanks (including whistle stops along the route). The state-owned railway offers several tour packages and provides excellent viewing opportunities from their popular dome cars. In accordance with recent Transportation Security Administration rules, passengers 18 years of age and older should be prepared to present a photo ID issued by a government authority along with two other forms of ID, one of which is issued by a government authority. *(See Websites, page 125, for contact information.)*

Wintery scene in Fairbanks

under the seemingly endless, and sometimes scorching, summer sun. At the annual summer-solstice celebration you can witness the Midnight Sun Baseball Game. If you are in Fairbanks in July, don't miss the **World Eskimo-Indian Olympics**, where indigenous athletes compete in traditional athletic games, dances, and pageants.

Fairbanks is the supply, transportation and medical services hub for Interior Alaska, as well as the jumping-off point for travel to more remote destinations. The Chena and Tanana Rivers meander through the birch, aspen, and spruce forests of the broad Tanana Valley, creating the perfect setting for wildlife viewing, camping, hiking, flightseeing, river rafting, canoeing, fishing, hunting, and more. The city is accessible by road via the Parks Highway (from Anchorage), or the Richard-son Highway (the last leg of the Alaska Highway). The Alaska Railroad offers daily summer service from Anchorage (with stops in Denali), and weekend service during winter. Three

Aurora borealis over Fairbanks

major airlines provide regularly scheduled flights into Fairbanks International Airport. Several regional or commuter carriers provide service from Canada or between Alaska communities.

Staff at the Fairbanks Convention and Visitors Bureau in the **Log Cabin Visitor Information Center** (550 First Avenue; open May–Sept daily 8am–8pm; winter Mon–Fri 8am–5pm) can answer your questions about what to see and do in the area, and offer maps and information about local tours. Satellite information booths are located at the Fairbanks International Airport and at the Alaska Railroad Depot. For questions regarding recreational opportunities on the area's public lands, stop at the nearby **Alaska Public Lands Information Center** (Courthouse Square, 250 Cushman Street, Suite 1A).

One unusual museum is the **Fairbanks Ice Museum** (in the historic Lacey Street Theater, 500 Second Avenue; open mid-May–late Sept 10am–8pm, hourly shows; admission charge). The museum shows a film detailing the history and spectacular ice carvings of the annual World Ice Art Championship held in February and March. You can also watch ice carvers in action as they create icy sculptures in this super-cool museum.

A stroll through the historic buildings and museums within the **Pioneer Park** (corner of Airport Way and Peger Road; open summer daily 11am–9pm; donations welcome) will educate you on the history of Fairbanks. In addition to the park's museums, you can visit the **Sternwheeler Nenana** (listed on the National Register of Historic Places), the **Alaska Native Village**, the **Alaska Salmon Bake** (summer 5–9pm), or catch a musical production on Fairbanks history at the **Palace Theater and Saloon** (summer daily 8.55pm; admission charge).

One of the highlights for many visitors to Fairbanks is a three-hour cruise on the Chena River aboard the **Riverboat Discovery** (1975 Discovery Drive; mid-May–mid-Sept daily 8:45am and 2pm; reservations required; admission charge). During the cruise you'll have a chance to watch a bush plane

---

Northern Lights

Alaska is the best place in the USA to view the aurora borealis, or northern lights. Literally meaning 'dawn of the north,' this is a solar-powered light show that occurs in the earth's upper atmosphere when charged particles from the sun collide with gas molecules.

The northern lights occur most intensely in an oval band that stretches across Alaska (as well as Canada, Greenland, Iceland, Norway, and Siberia). All the state, except parts of the southwest and the Aleutian Chain, are within the 'auroral zone,' with the best light shows visible north of the Alaska Range. One of the best views to be had is in Fairbanks, which calls itself an 'auroral destination,' in an attempt to lure winter visitors.

The aurora occurs throughout the year, but can be seen only on clear nights when the sky has darkened. In Alaska that means from fall through spring, with peak viewing in winter. Colors vary from pale yellowish green – the most common shade – to red, blue, and purplish-red. Northern lights often begin as long, uniform bands, stretching along the horizon, but may develop vertical bars or rays, that give the appearance of waving curtains. Some people claim they can not only see the aurora but can hear it as well. Scientists at the University of Alaska-Fairbanks, who have been studying the northern lights for years, are interested in such reports, but have yet to confirm them.

take off, meet a champion Iditarod musher, and learn about Athabascan Indian culture (at Chena Indian Village).

➤ The **University of Alaska's Museum of the North** (907 Yukon Drive; open mid-May–mid-Sept daily 9am–7pm; winter Mon–Fri 9am–5pm, Sat–Sun noon–5pm; admission charge) is often considered the best museum in Alaska. In the state's primary repository of natural and cultural history you see specimens that give an overview of the major regions of Alaska, as well as the culture and wildlife of the north. An interesting tour on the university campus is at the **Robert G. White Large Animal Research Station** (formerly the Musk-ox Farm; open late-May–early Sept daily 1.30 and 3.30pm; admission charge).

➤ Near the University (on College Road, behind the Alaska Department of Fish & Game) is the **Creamer's Field and Farmhouse Visitor Center** (open summer Mon–Fri 10am–5pm, Sat 10am–4pm). A dairy farm until 1966, Creamer's Field is now a waterfowl wildlife refuge for thousands of migratory birds, managed by the Alaska Department of Fish and Game. Viewing stations, located at various points along College Road, offer excellent vantage points, especially during spring and fall migrations. The refuge also has three nature trails that wind through forest, shrub, muskeg, and wetland habitats. Free, guided nature walks, lasting 1–2 hours, are conducted in summer (Wed and Sat 9am, Tues and Thur 7pm).

Around Fairbanks

Eight miles (13km) north of Fairbanks, on Steese Highway, is a **Trans-Alaska oil pipeline viewing station**. The Alyeska Pipeline Company offers tours and presentations at the **Fox Visitor Center** (early May–mid-Sept Mon–Sat 8am–6pm; free). Free tours of the pipeline are also offered at **Pump Station 9** (Richardson Highway, near Delta Junction).

Gold Dredge No. 8 (1755 Old Steese Highway) is said to be the only authentic Alaska dredge open to the public. Tours of the dredge and a chance to pan for gold are available (open mid-May–mid-Sept daily; hourly tours 9.30am–3.30pm; admission charge). Just north of the dredge is the **El Dorado Gold Mine** (Mile 1.3 Elliott Hwy, open mid-May–mid-Sept Sun–Fri, tours at 9.45am and 3pm, Sat 3pm; reservations required; admission charge). Tours include a ride on the Tanana Valley Railroad, a walking tour of a mining camp, and panning for gold. Another popular gold-mining attraction is a few miles west of Fairbanks: the **Ester Gold Mine Camp** (open late May–early Sept daily). Listed on the National Register of Historic Places, the camp was called Ester City in 1900. It has operated as a tourist attraction since 1958, offering lodging, meals, and shows includ-

Panning for gold

ing the Malamute Saloon Show (9pm nightly; admission charge) and the Northern Lights Photosymphony Show (6.45 and 7.45pm nightly; admission charge).

Children usually enjoy a short trip out of Fairbanks to the town of **North Pole** (13 miles/20km to the southeast on the Richardson Hwy) to shop for gifts and souvenirs at **Santa Claus House** (101 St Nicholas Drive; open May–Sept daily 8am–8pm; winter hours vary). Another great option is to treat yourself to a hot soak at **Chena Hot Springs Resort** (56 miles/90km from Fairbanks on the Chena Hot Springs

Road; open daily 7am–midnight; admission charge). Aside from indoor and outdoor pools fed by hot springs, you can arrange for lodging, massages, dog-sled tours, hiking, biking, canoeing, horseback riding, and more. In winter, there's excellent aurora borealis viewing, as well as skiing, snowshoeing, snowmachining, and, if you're hardy, a chance to sleep in a bed carved from ice (for registered guests of the hotel; significant additional charge), sit at an ice bar, and sip your drink from an ice martini glass at the **Aurora Ice Museum** (tours offered at 11am, 1pm, 3pm, 5pm, 7pm and 9pm; admission charge).

THE BUSH

When Alaskans refer to 'the Bush,' they are speaking of the communities in Alaska's rural areas, far from the road or rail systems, in the far north and southwest. Many residents of the Bush still live a traditional subsistence lifestyle, hunting, fishing, or mining the lands and waters surrounding their villages. However, Alaska Natives have now entered the cash economy, primarily through money and land received under the 1971 Alaska Native Claims Settlement Act *(see page 21)*. In many ways their lives still resemble those of their ancestors, yet now reflect the influences, both positive and negative, of the modern technology their new wealth affords. Telephones, Internet access, and satellite TV are common to most villages today, yet many still haul water (or chunks of ice) from fresh-water ponds into their homes, and 'honey buckets' (a bucket used as a toilet in rural homes lacking plumbing) are not uncommon. Native elders strive to pass on the ancient language, customs, skills, and values to the younger generation, who may be distracted by computer games or the next episode of 'Survivor.'

A trip to Bush Alaska is an exciting option for many visitors, but it requires special considerations. First of all, getting there. Transportation to the Bush is available by regional airlines and flight services from Anchorage or Fairbanks. Regional hub

Mileage marker, Barrow

cities within the Bush (Barrow, Kotzebue, Nome, Bethel, Dillingham, King Salmon, and Unalaska/Dutch Harbor) offer flights to outlying villages, but schedules may be variable and are always weather-dependent.

Second, bring money. The price of goods and services in the Bush is high, primarily due to staggering transportation costs. The shipment of a can of soup to a grocery store in the Bush may involve a ship, a plane, a truck, and an ATV. Any product with a limited shelf life is especially challenging to ship, difficult to preserve, and therefore expensive to buy. Lodging options for independent travelers must be carefully researched in advance. All the major hub cities have hotel and restaurant options. As you travel to more remote areas, however, the challenge of finding food and lodging becomes more pronounced.

Flexibility and a spirit of adventure will serve you well when visiting the Bush, and allow you to enjoy the chance of experiencing the landscape, wildlife, and cultures of remote Alaska.

Whale bones near Barrow

The Far North

This part of the Bush extends well above the Arctic Circle. Its centers of population – Barrow, Kotzebue, Nome – are some of the most isolated in the state

Barrow

Barrow is the northernmost community in North America, located on the coast of the Chukchi Sea, 10 miles (16km) south of Point Barrow and 340 miles (545km) north of the Arctic Circle. Sixty-four percent of the community's 4,400 residents are Native or part Native – mostly Inupiat Eskimos. Traditional subsistence hunting of marine mammals (whale, seal and walrus), polar bear, caribou, and duck, as well as fishing for grayling and whitefish are still an important part of the local culture. Most residents, however, have homes heated by the natural gas of nearby fields, and equipped with electricity, water, and sewer systems. Barrow is the economic center of the North Slope Borough, the city's primary employer. The Wiley Post-Will Rogers Memorial Airport is the regional transportation center for the area. Barrow is served by regularly scheduled commercial flights from Anchorage and Fairbanks.

Visitors traveling to **Barrow** are often drawn by the famed midnight sun. From May 10 to August 2, the sun does not set in Barrow. Conversely, darkness reigns from November 18 through January 24 (67 days). The darkness, and the flat, treeless landscape allow for spectacular displays of the aurora borealis, a good reason to visit during winter. Other motivations include standing on the northernmost point on the continent, experiencing traditional whaling festivals, or looking (carefully) for polar bears. Additional resident wildlife includes grizzly bears, arctic and red foxes, moose, caribou, wolves, Dall sheep, snowy owls, whales, and bearded, ringed, and spotted seals. Birders travel to the area in spring and summer to view the more than 250 bird species nesting in the area.

The **Inupiat Heritage Center** (5421 North Star Street; open Mon–Fri 8.30am–5pm; admission charge) has exhibits on the history, language and culture of the Inupiat people, plus traditional skills workshops and Native crafts sales.

Kotzebue

Kotzebue (population 3,100) is located on the Baldwin Peninsula in Kotzebue Sound, 26 miles (42km) north of the Arctic Circle. Its location, near the discharges of the Kobuk,

Grocery shopping in Kotzebue

Noatak, and Selawik rivers, made the area the hub of ancient arctic trading routes. Today, Kotzebue continues to be the center for service and transportation for villages in the northwest region of Alaska. Regularly scheduled airline service to Kozebue is available from Anchorage via Nome.

Kotzebue residents are primarily Inupiat Eskimos, and most still live a subsistence lifestyle. Visit the **North Tent City**, a traditional fish camp set up each summer to dry and smoke the season's catch. A stroll down Front Street (the water front) will take you past fishing boats, and fish drying on racks in the traditional Eskimo style.

The **Innaigvik Education and Information Center** (open May–Sept daily 8am–5pm) can provide you with information on the various public lands accessed from Kotzebue.

Nome

Historic **Nome** lies by the Bering Sea on Seward Peninsula's southern edge. Its 3,500 residents (a little over half of whom are Native or part Native) live 102 miles (164km) south of the Arctic Circle, and 161 miles (259km) east of Russia. The city's beginnings date back to 1898, when three 'Lucky Swedes,' Jafet Lindeberg, Erik Lindblom, and John Brynteson made

Mosquitoes and other Pests

One of the most important things to remember to bring along on your trip to Alaska is insect repellent with a high percentage of Deet. Alaska is famous for its giant mosquitoes, often called the Alaska State Bird. But it's no joke when your outdoor adventure is spoiled by them, or by no-see-ums (tiny, flying terrors), or other biting insects. If your travel takes you away from the cities and into the backcountry, bring head nets or 'bug jackets' along, and plan to wear long trousers and long-sleeved shirts made of thick material. Mosquitoes can bite through thin fabric.

a $1,500-to-the-pan gold discovery on tiny Anvil Creek. The area became a tent-and-log-cabin town of 20,000 miners, saloon-keepers, and scoundrels, seemingly overnight. Thousands of additional prospectors swarmed to the area, armed with shovels, buckets, gold pans, and rockers. Within two months, over $1 million in gold had been gleaned from the sands of Nome. Since the first strike on Anvil Creek, $136 million in gold has come from the town's gold fields.

Nome River

Not all of Nome's history has been golden, however. The area has suffered from violent storms, devastating fires, and a major influenza epidemic. In 1925 the region was threatened with a diphtheria epidemic, prompting dog mushers to relay 300,000 units of life-saving serum from Nenana to Nome. The annual Iditarod Trail Sled Dog Race *(see page 50)* commemorates that heroic achievement.

Nome is the supply, service, and transportation center of the Bering Strait region. A commercial airline supplies regularly scheduled passenger and cargo service to the city from Anchorage and Fairbanks. Over 20,000 visitors come to Nome yearly, many to enjoy the longest day of the year, June 21, with sunrise at 3.59am and sunset at 12.48am. Other, hardier souls may choose to visit during the winter solstice, December 21, when the sun reluctantly rises at 12.03pm and hurries to set at

3.57pm. One of the most popular reasons for visiting Nome is to stand at the finish line of the Iditarod in mid-March.

Visitors to Nome may take a self-guided historical walking tour, or rent a car and drive the 300 miles (482km) of local roads (watching for bear, moose, reindeer, and musk oxen along the way). Other popular activities include bird-watching, fishing, hunting, panning for gold, or (in late March) playing a round of golf on the frozen Bering Sea. Learn more about the gold rush, Native culture, and the history of the Iditarod at the **Carrie M. McLain Memorial Museum** (223 Front Street; open June–Sept daily 10am–6pm; winter noon–6pm; free). The headquarters of the **Bering Land Bridge National Preserve** (a rarely visited national park unit covering much of the Seward Peninsula north of Nome) is located on Front Street, and is a great source for wilderness information.

The Southwest

Southwest Alaska takes in the Bush communities of Bethel, Dillingham, and King Salmon – all located relatively close to the Bering Sea. Where the Alaska Peninsula ends, the Aleutian Islands begin; Unalaska is the chain's busy center.

Bethel

The central hub for the villages of southwest Alaska is the city of **Bethel**, located at the mouth of the Kuskokwim River, 40 miles (64km) inland from the Bering Sea. Bethel has served as a regional trading, transportation, and distribution center since the early 1900s. Today it is a city of nearly 6,000 people, almost 70 percent of whom are Native or part Native. The Bethel Airport is the third-busiest airport in Alaska, serving 56 villages of the Yukon-Kuskokwim Delta.

There are roughly 26 miles (42km) of roads in Bethel, only a few of them paved. In winter, however, the State of Alaska maintains an ice road *on* the Kuskokwim River that can exceed 100 miles (160km) in length. Daily commercial flights are available from Anchorage to Bethel, as well as scheduled (or chartered) air-taxi service to outlying villages.

➤ The **Yupiit Piciryarait Cultural Center and Museum** (420 Chief Eddie Hoffman Highway; open Tues–Fri 1.30–4.30pm; donation requested) contains exhibits detailing the area's ancient and contemporary Eskimo and Athabascan cultures.

Bethel lies within the boundaries of the **Yukon Delta National Wildlife Refuge**. The refuge visitor center (807 Chief Eddie

Sea otters taking a bath

Hoffman Highway) provides information on the recreational, wildlife viewing, birding, hunting, and fishing opportunities available. Access to the refuge is generally by small plane, and will likely be expensive.

Dillingham

The city of **Dillingham**, located on Nushagak Bay at the mouth of the Wood and Nushagak rivers, started out as a Russian trade center in 1818, drawing local Natives (as well as those from the Kuskokwim region, the Alaska Peninsula and Cook Inlet) to the trading-post area. In 1837, a Russian Orthodox mission was established, and by 1884 the first Bristol Bay cannery was constructed – followed by 10 additional canneries built within the next two decades. Dillingham was incorporated as a city in 1963.

Today, Dillingham (population 2,400) is the center of economic, transportation, and public services for the western Bristol Bay region. Local economy is primarily based on commercial fishing, though many residents also depend on subsistence hunting and fishing, as well as the income derived from trapping. Dillingham's waterways are famous for hearty runs of all five species of salmon, plus arctic char, grayling, northern pike, lake trout, and dolley varden. Moose, caribou, and bears are among the land mammals common to the area, and Beluga or orca whales can be seen along the coast during salmon runs. **Wood-Tikchik State Park**, **Togiak National Wildlife Refuge**, and **Walrus Islands State Game Sanctuary** are all public lands that can be accessed from Dillingham.

Many Dillingham residents depend on fishing

The **Sam Fox Museum** (located in the library building, ◄ 306 D Street West; open Mon–Fri noon–4pm; donations welcome) features exhibits of Native artifacts, clothing, and crafts as well as information on the Bristol Bay commercial fishery. Dillingham offers various outdoor recreation options including hiking, boating, kayaking, and rafting.

King Salmon

In 1912, Mount Katmai (on the Alaska Peninsula) erupted, forcing the Native people living nearby to seek safer surroundings. They chose to relocate their village, now known as **King Salmon**, to the banks of the Naknek River, about 15 miles (24km) from Kvichak Bay. The United States Government constructed an air-force base in the area at the beginning of World War II, and in 1949 added a post office and a road to the nearby coastal community of Naknek. The base went into caretaker status in 1993, though it is still used to support daily military activities, as well as offices of the Bristol Bay Borough and the State of Alaska.

Today, the community of King Salmon is classified as an 'isolated village' by the state. Most of the 400 residents (30 percent of whom are Alaska Native or part Native) now live in modern, wood-framed homes.

King Salmon is an important transportation area for the Bristol Bay commercial salmon fishery, and a departure point for **McNeil River State Game Sanctuary**, **Brooks Camp**, and **Valley of Ten Thousand Smokes**, all within **Katmai National Park and Preserve**.

Information about the park is available at the National Park Service's **King Salmon Visitor Center** (next to the airport; open June–Aug daily 8am–5pm, Sept–May Tues–Sat 8am–5pm). Additionally, several remote lodges in the area provide flightseeing, wildlife viewing, and sport-fishing adventures (rainbow trout and all five species of salmon).

St Paul Island, the tiniest of Alaska's remote Pribilof Islands, located 300 miles (482km) west of the mainland in the frigid Bering Sea, is a paradise for birders. In May, strong winds from the west occasionally blast a variety of Asian vagrants (including Far Eastern curlew, common snipe, and the Siberian rubythroat) hundreds of miles off their migration routes and into the binocular view of awe-struck bird-watchers.

King Salmon is accessible by scheduled jet and charter flights from Anchorage.

For a list of lodges and tour operators in the King Salmon area (and throughout Alaska), contact the Alaska Travel Industry Association (2600 Cordova Street, Suite 201, Anchorage AK 99503; or check <www.travelalaska.com>).

The Aleutian Chain: Unalaska

The city of **Unalaska** is located on two islands on the Aleutian Chain (Unalaska and Amaknak islands), connected, since 1980, by a bridge. The city overlooks two bodies of water, Ilioliuk Bay and Dutch Harbor. Over time, the portion of the city located on Amaknak Island has come to be called 'Dutch Harbor,' although it is within the boundaries of the City of Unalaska. Commercial airlines also generally refer to the entire community as 'Dutch Harbor,' which is something to remember when making flight arrangements.

The history of Unalaska is colorful, varied and often tragic. It is a story of self-reliance, invasion, greed, abuse, internment, resourcefulness, and resilience. Today, that resourcefulness and resilience has resulted in a bustling port city (population 4,400) that is the center of the Bering Sea fishing industry and the hub, or crossroads, of the Aleutians. The local economy is based on the seafood industry and fleet services. Access to Unalaska is through regularly scheduled commercial flights from Anchorage, or by an Alaska Marine

Highway System ferry or cruise ship. Sport fishing, beach-combing, hiking, kayaking, and wildlife viewing among the available recreational activities.

The **Museum of the Aleutians** (314 Salmon Way; open June–Sept Mon–Sat 11am–4pm, Sun noon–5pm; winter Tues–Sat 11am–4pm; admission charge) displays artifacts from archeological digs, World War II relics, and contemporary artwork. Next door to the museum is the **Ounalashka Corporation** (a non-profit Native corporation), which owns much of the land in Unalaska. Stop by their offices (400 Salmon Way) to obtain recreational land-use permits (for a nominal fee), visit their cultural library and Native art display, and get information on the **Aleutian World War II National Historic Area** (at Ulakhta Head, on Airport Beach Road). Anyone interested in history will be drawn to this, as well as numerous other World War II military sites on the islands. Birdwatchers will enjoy opportunities to observe rare species, especially those unique to the Aleutians.

For more information on attractions and tours of Unalaska (or Dutch Harbor) visit the **Unalaska/Port of Dutch Harbor Convention and Visitors Bureau** (in the former World War II Burma Road Chapel, on the corner of Fifth and Broadway) or go to <www.unalaska.info>.

A net full of salmon

WHAT TO DO

Alaska is a place for the adventurous, as well as those who simply want to admire its awe-inspiring scenery. Some people come here for the express purpose of conquering Mount McKinley, the tallest peak in North America. Others prefer to gaze on it from the dome car of a passing Alaska Railroad train. Hearty backcountry hikers can be dropped off by bush plane for a month of solitude in the remote Gates of the Arctic National Park, raft the mighty Yukon River, or surf the frigid breakers off the beach of Yakatat. Other visitors may choose to stroll through botanical gardens, take a ride on a Fairbanks riverboat, or soak their cares away at Chena Hot Springs. Regardless of your goals, skills, or stamina, Alaska offers a wide range of recreational options.

> **For details on activities, equipment rentals, tour operators, outfitters, guides, and more, check with the Convention and Visitors Bureau closest to your destination (*see page 122*).**

Alaska also offers cultural activities – the performing arts are well represented – and opportunities to shop for Native-made arts and crafts, as well as some festivals that have no equivalent anywhere in the world.

OUTDOOR ACTIVITIES

Water activities. Many activities involve water, as most communities are close to the sea or inland waterways. Boating, canoeing, kayaking, river rafting, and wildlife cruises are available at almost every Alaska destination. If wild waters call to you, Alaska has a total of 26 waterways that have

Camping on top of the world

been designated as National Wild and Scenic Rivers due to their wilderness characteristics and recreational opportunities. Access must be by chartered Bush plane, as these rivers are far from the road system. The Federal Aviation Administration of the US prohibits pilots from lashing canoes or kayaks to the pontoons of floatplanes while carrying passengers; inflatable rafts and folding canvas or rubber kayaks are more convenient and less expensive to take along. You can learn more about these rivers from the Alaska Public Lands Information Center *(see page 122)*.

Hunting. Hunters head for Alaska in search of black, brown (or grizzly) bear, bison, caribou, moose, goat, musk-ox, or Dall sheep. The State of Alaska Department of Fish and Game should be contacted for information on specific area regulations and licensing (<www.sf.adfg.state.ak.us>).

Camping. If camping is what you had in mind, Alaska has endless possibilities, from roadside campgrounds (with RV hookups, tent sites, on-site drinking water, firewood, and outhouses) to fly-in, remote camping. Hiking trails and backpacking opportunities run the same gamut: from a short

Fishing

If you're more interested in fishing Alaska waters than traversing them, world-class sport-fishing opportunities are available throughout Alaska for species including arctic char, trout, burbot, grayling, rockfish, lingcod, whitefish, sheefish, halibut, and all five species of Pacific salmon. Fishing licenses are available at almost all sporting-goods stores, most variety stores, and at several grocery stores. Anyone aged 16 or older must have a fishing license when angling on Alaska's waters; that includes both fresh and saltwater. For regulations and licensing information contact the Alaska Division of Sportfish on (907) 465-4100 or <www.state.ak.us/adfg/adfghome.htm>.

Hiking trail outside Juneau

morning climb up Flattop Mountain in Anchorage to arduous treks through any of Alaska's wilderness areas. The Alaska Public Lands offices *(see page 122)* have all the information you need.

Summer sports. Summer spectator sports include baseball (Alaska has six baseball semi-pro or collegiate teams) and the World Eskimo-Indian Olympics (held in Fairbanks in July).

Winter sports. As you might expect, winter sports are big in Alaska and include ice-skating, skiing, ski-joring, snow boarding, snowshoeing, sledding, snow-machining, ice fishing, ice climbing, and even curling (in Fairbanks). If you prefer indoor pursuits, join the winter-sports spectators at collegiate basketball tournaments and ice hockey games.

Sled dogs. Sled-dog racing is the official state sport of Alaska. Long-distance racers compete in events like the 1,100-mile (1,770-km) Iditarod Trail Sled Dog Race or the 1,000-mile (1,610-km) Yukon Quest International Sled Dog

Race. Short-distance sprint racing events are also popular, with yearly races held in Southcentral and Interior Alaska.

Other activities. If you entertain loftier ideas for exploring Alaska, flightseeing tours (for viewing glaciers, wildlife, Mount McKinley, and more) are available throughout the state by small plane, floatplane, helicopter, and even (in Fairbanks) hot-air balloon. Other ways of touring the state include motorcycles, all-terrain vehicles and dogsleds (even in summer on glaciers or mountains).

SHOPPING

If shopping is your idea of recreation, Alaska has a lot to offer. Major cities have shopping malls with national chain stores. For souvenirs and gifts, go to the smaller gift shops, museums, and art galleries that feature local or Native-made arts and crafts. Pay special attention to labels: the 'Made in Alaska' symbol of a mother polar bear and cub means the product was made in Alaska. The 'Silver Hand' symbol that says, 'Authentic Native Handcraft from Alaska,' means the item was made by a member of a recognized tribe, or a certified Indian artisan. Authentic articles bought direct from craftsmen, or in remote villages, do not have a symbol attached. Check with the Convention and Visitors Bureaus for the best sources of authentic Native arts and crafts.

Federal laws require permits to export certain Native crafts (made of the skins of protected mammals). The simplest solution is to have the store ship the items, insured, to your home address. If not, to take Alaska wildlife products out of the country you need a permit from the US Fish and Wildlife Service in Anchorage, a process that may take a few days. For a marine-mammal product, the permit must come from the Washington, DC office, and will take up to a month to receive (for information, contact the US Fish and Wildlife Service in Anchorage, tel: 907-271-6198).

ENTERTAINMENT

The performing arts are well represented in larger cities by music, dance, and theater productions. From classical concerts to folk-festival fiddling; from ballet to Native dance performances, the full range of Alaskan lifestyles is reflected. Convention and Visitors Bureaus will have information on concerts, gallery events, and theatre productions in the larger cities. The following is a sampling of what's on offer.

Juneau's Perseverance Theatre (914 Third Street) is a non-profit regional theater that specializes in producing new and classic works, viewed from an Alaska perspective.

In **Anchorage**, the **Alaska Center for the Performing Arts** (**pac**; W. Sixth Avenue), is the place for Anchorage Symphony Orchestra, Anchorage Opera, and Anchorage Dance Company performances, as well as those of internationally

Malamute Saloon show in Ester Gold Camp

acclaimed artists in dance, music, and theater. **Cyrano's Off Center Playhouse** (413 D St), a coffee shop/bookstore/theater, features first-rate productions in a casual atmosphere.

The **Fairbanks Concert Association** sponsors musical, dance, and theatrical presentations at the Hering Auditorium (901 Fairbanks Way). In November, Fairbanks hosts the **Athabascan Fiddlers Festival** at the Chena River Convention Center.

NIGHTLIFE

'Nightlife' in Alaska may have a slightly different connotation than in other locales. Due to the extended (in many cases 24-hour) summer daylight, nightlife can look pretty much like 'daylife.' Fishing, camping, golfing, hiking, hunting, or gardening can go on regardless of the hour, and they often do. At the Fairbanks Country Club, for example, you can reserve a tee time 24 hours a day in June and July. The converse is true for winter – in Barrow, for example, nightlife consists of everything you do.

Alaska does have its share of bars, clubs, and nightspots, many with a distinctive Alaska flair. The following is a sampling of the types of establishments found in the major cities.

The Red Dog Saloon (278 S. Franklin Street) in **Juneau** is a fun, though decidedly touristy, bar, complete with swinging doors, a sawdust-strewn floor, and mining memorabilia.

The nightlife in **Anchorage** includes **Humpy's Great Alaska Ale House** (610 W. Sixth Avenue), a casual downtown alehouse that has great beer, savory food, reasonable prices, live local music, and (for sports fans) a wide-screen TV. If you would like to have some tasty gourmet pizza and award-winning beer, head over to the **Moose's Tooth Pub and Pizzeria** (3300 Old Seward Highway). At the **Bear Tooth Theaterpub and Grill** (1230 W. 27th Avenue, just off Spenard Road) you can enjoy food, wine or beer, movies, live music, and more. If you're looking for a humorous take on life in Alaska, **Mr Whitekey's Fly by Night Club** (3300 Spenard Road) features live music, dancing, and rowdy shows like the 'Whale Fat Follies,' with desserts and beverages to go with them. **Chilkoot Charlie's** (2435 Spenard Road) is a popular, raucous, Alaska-themed bar that's known for a variety of live entertainment, sawdust floors, three stages, three dance floors, and 10 bars (11 in summer).

In **Fairbanks**, the **Blue Loon** (2999 Parks Highway) has beer, sandwiches, appetizers, live music, and movies. For vaudeville-type music and comedy stage shows (loosely based on Alaska's history), visit the **Palace Theater and Saloon** in Pioneer Park (corner of Airport Way and Peger Road); or the **Malamute Saloon** in Ester Gold Camp (7 miles/12km west of Fairbanks). The **Café Alex Wine Bar** (310 First Avenue) has a quieter atmosphere with wine, appetizers, and piano music. You can enjoy light food and drinks at **Pike's Landing** (Mile 4.5 Airport Road). Pike's deck overlooking the Chena River is a good setting for a pleasant evening under the midnight sun. Located in a historic building, the **Pump House** (Mile 1.3 Chena Pump Road) features seafood and steak. The bar is a popular nightspot for the younger crowd.

Juneau fireworks

CHILDREN'S ALASKA

One of the great facets of a family vacation to Alaska is that children can join in almost every activity – wildlife viewing, camping, hiking, fishing, sightseeing, and more. Getting them to sleep at night under bright summer sunlight may take a bit of doing. Be sure to bring along plenty of mosquito repellent and sunscreen.

Trips aboard the **Alaska Marine Highway System** ferries are fun for children. Most ferries offer cafeterias, play areas (for young children), video games, and various lounges, rooms, and decks for exploration. Kids also enjoy excursions aboard the **Alaska Railroad** (routes available between Seward and Fairbanks) or the **White Pass Yukon Route Railroad** trip from Skagway to the 2,865-ft (873-m) White Pass.

In Anchorage, favorite activities for children include a visit to the **Imaginarium Science Discovery Center**, a hands-on science exploration museum, a trip to **Alaska Zoo**, and picnics at city parks and playgrounds. Other Anchorage options include renting bicycles and riding the **Tony Knowles Coastal Trail**, or a trip to the indoor water park, **H2Oasis** *(see page 46)*. Just south of Anchorage, near Portage, children can get a close-up look at wild animals at the **Alaska Wildlife Conservation Center** *(see page 52)*. Traveling further south to Seward, a tour of the **Alaska Sealife Center** and a wildlife cruise into the **Kenai Fjords National Park** are fun and educational highlights for everyone *(see page 57)*.

Fairbanks festival

Calendar of Events

January Polar Bear Jump Off (Seward), Sled-dog races, Winterfest, Russian Christmas.

February Alaska Airlines Winter Classics, Anchorage Fur Rendezvous, Yukon Quest International and World Championship sled-dog races, snow-machine races.

March Iditarod Trail Sled Dog Race, Fairbanks Winter Carnival and World Ice Art Championship, Bering Sea Ice Golf Classic (Nome).

April Native Youth Olympics (Anchorage), Alyeska Spring Carnival and Slush Cup, Kodiak Whalefest, Valdez extreme winter sports.

May Copper River Delta (Cordova) and Kachemak Bay (Homer) Shore-bird Festivals, Kodiak King Crab Festival, Petersburg's Little Norway Festival.

June Mayor's Midnight Sun Marathon (Anchorage), Highland Games (Chugiak/Eagle River), Nalukataq Whaling Festival (Barrow), Midnight Sun Baseball Game (Fairbanks), Gold Rush Days (Juneau), Colony Days (Palmer), Sitka Music Festival, summer solstice celebrations.

July Mount Marathon Race (Seward), Fourth of July celebrations, World Eskimo-Indian Olympics (Fairbanks), Forest Faire (Girdwood), Fishtival (Naknek), Talkeetna Moose Dropping Festival.

August State fairs, Unalaska Tundra Golf Classic, Talkeetna Bluegrass Festival.

September Klondike Road Rally (Skagway), Great Alaska Quilt Show (Anchorage), Kodiak State Fair and Rodeo, Alaska Airlines Autumn Classics.

October Hockey tournaments (Anchorage), Petersburg Oktoberfest Artshare, Sitka Alaska Day Festival, Murder on the Alaska Railroad Excursion (Wasilla).

November Great Alaska Shootout (Anchorage), Athabascan Fiddlers Festival, Top of the World Classic, Haines Bald Eagle Festival.

December Christmas festivals, Colony Christmas Parade and Fair (Palmer), Holiday Train (Seward), Talkeetna Bachelor Society Ball and Wilderness Woman Contest.

EATING OUT

Make this a rule: when eating out in Alaska, don't ever pass up the chance to dine on genuine, fresh local seafood. King crab, wild salmon, halibut, clams, oysters, and mussels, all fresh from the sea, skillfully prepared by local chefs, and whisked to your table, can redefine how excellent seafood is really supposed to taste. Even if you're not convinced you care for fish, Alaska chefs may well win you over.

The state's restaurants also offer a wide range of beef, pork, or chicken dishes, as well as a variety of savory vegetarian options. Restaurants specializing in Greek, Italian, Chinese, Thai, Japanese, Korean, Indian, Mexican, and Cajun cuisines are among the many delicious choices that await you.

Breakfast

Your first decision of the day will probably involve breakfast. Many hotels in Alaska offer early-morning complimentary breakfasts for their guests. These meals will include coffee, tea, fruit juices, milk, breads, pastries, cereal, yogurt, and possibly eggs, waffles, pancakes, or French toast. Hotel restaurants also generally have full breakfast menus that will include all of the above, and add meat (maybe reindeer, Italian, German, or other breakfast sausages, steak, bacon, or ham), egg dishes (specialty omelets or boiled, poached, scrambled, or fried eggs) and fruit plates. You should remem-

> **Wild Copper River king, red, and silver salmon are famous throughout the world for their rich color, firm texture and mouth-watering flavor.**

Natives of Alaska still dry their salmon for use during the winter

ber that, unless the menu specifies that the fruit is 'fresh', you will likely find fruit toppings – say for your pancakes or waffles – to be of the frozen variety. Various family-style restaurants offer hearty breakfasts that can be ordered at any time from early morning to very late at night. Plus, nearly every Alaska town has a favorite spot, a small diner or café, that is popular with locals residents for having good coffee (with free re-fills), generous breakfasts, and friendly service.

You might check to see if your hotel desk clerk actually lives in Alaska (many summer workers within the tourism industry are from outside of Alaska), and if so, get their recommendation. Sunday brunches are often an option in hotels and restaurants, and offer a wide variety of break-fast and lunch choices in an all-you-can-eat buffet. A word of warning – these brunches can become very busy with the arrival of the after-church crowd.

Lunch

When it comes to lunch-time decisions, you'll discover that larger Alaska cities generally have a number of upscale cafés, steakhouse grills or trendy brewpubs. Their lunch menus are often similar to their dinnertime options, but the quantities and prices are usually less. In addition, family-style restaurants offer specialty burgers, barbecued ribs, sandwiches, salads, and more. Of course the standard fast-food burger and fries, tacos, fried chicken, hot dogs, or bratwurst (or the not-so-standard rein-deer sausage) fare is readily available in all the major population areas, if you're so busy fishing or seeing the sights that you can't take the time for a more leisurely restaurant meal. One dish you cannot purchase at any Alaska restaurant is a moose steak. Federal law prohibits the sale of wild game meats, so to sample moose, bear, or caribou, you'll need to get yourself invited to dinner at the home of a successful Alaska hunter.

Alaska King crab

If you happen to be in Alaska for the Independence Day celebrations on the Fourth of July, you're in luck. Nearly every city and town has festivities that will likely include sumptuous barbecues of fresh salmon and halibut, and, per-haps, an opportunity to sample wild game.

Dinner

In Alaska, as in other US cities, the major meal of the day is enjoyed in the evening (with the exception of Sunday, when lunch is usually the main meal). Visitors are often delighted to discover that there is fine dining to be had in Alaska's main centers of population. While there are probably fewer qualifying restaurants than in the average city in the Lower 48 (states), you may be pleasantly surprised by the selection and quality of entrees, excellent service and sophisticated (by Alaska standards) atmosphere. An added bonus is that dress codes are more relaxed – jackets and ties are generally not required.

As you move away from the larger cities and venture into smaller, more isolated communities, you'll still find various restaurant options, but the selection may be limited, the cuisine 'eclectic', and the cost impressive. Dining at a restaurant in a small community will, however, afford an excellent opportunity to mix with the local people, peruse small-town newspapers, and soak up the atmosphere. Plus, if a small community restaurant has a sudden rush, locals

Special Occasions

Holidays in Alaska, like other places in the world, are times for getting together with family. However, a disproportionate number of Alaska's residents – many of whom arrive in the state due to military service or other job-related reasons – do not have extended family living nearby. When special holidays, such as Thanksgiving (the fourth Thursday in November), roll around, Alaskans often gather at a close friend's home to enjoy a special dinner (oven-roasted turkey, sage dressing, mashed potatoes, gravy, vegetables, salads, rolls, cranberry sauce, pies…) with their Alaska 'family,' to count their blessings, and reflect on past Thanksgiving dinners with loved ones in far-away places.

may jump up, bus the tables and bring you your food, just to help out. That's Alaska.

Sweet

A sweet addition to any trip to Anchorage or Homer can be found at Alaska Wild Berry Products, 5225 Juneau Street, or in the Fifth Avenue Mall in Anchorage (or 528 East Pioneer Street in Homer), where various wild berries, hand-picked from throughout the state, have been made into a tasty array of jams, jellies, candies, syrups, and sauces. Gift packs are available. At the main store in Anchorage, you'll see 'the world's tallest chocolate fall,' a 20-ft (6-m) high fountain flowing with 3,400lb (1,500kg) of melted milk chocolate.

Low bush cranberries

It is often said that the people of Alaska consume the largest amount of ice cream, per capita, in the USA. Whether it's stopping by the local ice-cream vendor for a single cone of self-indulgence, or bringing home a half-gallon of your favorite flavor to share with friends and family, ice cream does seem to hit the spot with Alaskans, even when enjoyed beside a cozy fire on a long winter evening.

What to Drink

Alaskans also know how to quench a thirst. Water, straight from the tap, is delicious in Alaska, and almost always served along with your meals. The coffee is robust, especially those local brands roasted within the state: Café del

At a microbrewery

Mundo, Kaladi Brothers, Ravens Brew, Alaska Coffee Roasting Company, or Heritage Coffee. You don't even have to go to a restaurant to enjoy great coffee here, because roadside kiosks are everywhere (in larger cities), selling brewed coffees, designer espressos, Italian sodas, blender drinks, plus delicious, and (quick) lunch options. Some will even give your dog a treat.

Another thirst quencher is Alaska-brewed beer. Brewpubs and microbreweries are located throughout the state. Anchorage: Glacier Brewhouse, 737 W. Fifth Avenue; Midnight Sun Brewing Company, 7329 Arctic Boulevard; The Moose's Tooth, 3300 Old Seward Highway; Sleeping Lady Brewery, 717 W. Third Avenue. Fox (near Fairbanks): Silver Gulch Brewing and Bottling, 2195 Old Steese Highway. Haines: Haines Brewing Company, 108 White Fang Way (Dalton City). Homer: Homer Brewing Company, 1411 Lake Shore. Juneau: Alaskan Brewing, 5429 Shaune Drive.

HANDY TRAVEL TIPS

An A–Z Summary of Practical Information

A

ACCOMMODATIONS *(see also the list of* RECOMMENDED HOTELS *starting on page 126)*

Accommodation is generally expensive in Alaska, especially during the peak tourist season (mid-May to mid-September), when it is always a good idea to book hotel rooms several months in advance. The range of hotels in Anchorage, by far the largest city, includes a hostel, many, varied B&Bs, private, or chain hotels (representing a wide range of costs and amenities), and the luxury Hotel Captain Cook. Other major cities, like Fairbanks and Juneau, while offering fewer choices than Anchorage, still have a good variety of options. Even smaller cities that enjoy a bustling tourist economy, like Ketchikan (and others in Southeast), Seward, or Talkeetna, have excellent, modern hotels with rustic décor. When you venture farther out into village communities, lodging options remain expensive, and may be decidedly less luxurious and far more 'creative.' Check the Recommended Hotels section, or contact local Convention and Visitors Bureaus *(see pages 122–4)* for a more complete listing.

Youth Hostels

A number of Alaska cities have hostels that range from basic and utilitarian to warm and inviting. Some have 24-hour access; many have good storage facilities and Internet access; some have a no-smoking and/or no-alcohol policy. Among the best are:

   The Spenard Hostel International (2845 W 42 Ave, Anchorage 99517, tel: 907-248-5036, <www.AlaskaHostel.org>.

   Billie's Backpackers' Hostel (2895 Mack Blvd, Fairbanks, tel: 907-479-2034, <www.Alaskahostel.com>).

   GoNorth Hostel (3500 Davis Rd, PO Box 60147, Fairbanks 99706, tel: 866-236-7272 or 907-479-7272, <www.paratours.net>.

   The **Homer Hostel** (304 W. Pioneer Ave, Homer 99603, tel: 907-235-1463, <www.homerhostel.com>).

Juneau International Hostel (614 Harris St, Juneau 99801, tel: 907-586-9559, <www.juneauhostel.org>).

The **Alaska Island Hostel** (805 Gjoa St, Petersburg 99833, tel: 907-772-3632 or 907-723-5340, <www.alaskaislandhostel.com>).

The **Moby Dick Hostel** (423 3rd Ave, PO Box 624, Seward 99664, tel: 907-224-7072, <www.mobydickhostel.com>).

The **Skagway Home Hostel** (3rd Ave near Main St, PO Box 231 Skagway 99840, tel: 907-983-2131, <www.skagwayhostel.com>).

AIRPORTS

Anchorage's **Ted Stevens International Airport** is the primary entry hub for Alaska. It is served by several major domestic carriers (more in summer than in winter), which include **Alaska**, **American**, **America West**, **Northwest**, **Delta**, **United**, and **Continental Airlines**. Alaska Airlines offers by far the most flights to and within Alaska. International carriers include **Air Canada**, **Condor**, **Asiana**, **Cathay Pacific**, **China**, **Korean**, and **Mavial/Magadan Airlines**. Several regional carriers fly from Ted Stevens (and from **Merrill Field**, east of downtown) to smaller communities.

Ted Stevens International has two terminals, the north for international flights, and the south for domestic. Baggage and freezer storage (a consideration for hunters and fishers) is available on the lower level of the domestic terminal. Free shuttle service provided between the two terminals, and to many local hotels (telephone information board in baggage-claim area). The Municipality of Anchorage People Mover buses offer public transportation from the airport (both terminals) to the Dimond Center (a large mall in south Anchorage) or downtown. Car rental is available at the airport, as are taxis and vehicle-for-hire van service for larger groups.

Fairbanks International Airport serves as the hub for travelers headed to Alaska's Interior. **Alaska Airlines** provides year-round service to Fairbanks. **Northwest** and **Delta Airlines** offer flights during the summer only. Weekly service between Fairbanks and Frankfurt is available through **Thomas Cook** (via **Condor**). Regional airlines provide transportation from Fairbanks into smaller, outlying cities and towns of the Interior and the Bush.

Alaska Airlines also provides daily service to many Southeast communities. Don't assume that free shuttle service will be available at these smaller Alaska airports. Ketchikan International Airport, for example, is on Gravina Island. To get to Revillagigedo Island, where the city of Ketchikan is located, you'll need to carry your luggage from the airport, down a walkway to the nearby dock, and take a short ferry ride across the Tongass Narrows. Taxi service is available once you're there – if you've arranged it in advance.

B

BUDGETING FOR YOUR TRIP

The expense of traveling in Alaska is surprising to some. Here's a list of the average, approximate prices in US dollars when this book went to press (2005).

Camping. One of the cheaper options. Federal and state-run campsites cost $6–$24 per night. Reserve in advance.

Hotels. See Recommended Hotels for price range.

Meals. See Recommended Restaurants for price range.

Transportation. (See also Airports.) Most cities and even small towns offer taxi service. In Anchorage, a cab from the airport to downtown costs about $20, excluding tips, which are expected by drivers. Larger Alaska cities provide bus services. In Anchorage, a trip on the city bus (The People Mover) costs $1.50 a trip, or $3 a day for unlimited travel. The People Mover has 15 regular routes, plus four Dart (Dial-a-Ride-Transit) routes. Kids go free on Thursday in summer. A *Ride Guide* containing route maps (and much more) is available at local stores, visitor centers, and other locations.

Attractions. A sample of prices for attractions within the Anchorage area is as follows: **Anchorage Zoo** ($9 adults/$5 children), **H2Oasis** indoor waterpark ($19.95 adults/$15.95 children), the **Alaska Native Heritage Center** ($21 adults/$16 children), the **Imaginarium** science discovery center ($5.50 adults/$5 children), and the **Alaska Experience Center** ($10 adults/$7 children). Seward's **Alaska SeaLife Center** ($14 adults/$11 children) and day cruises into **Kenai Fjords National Park** ($70–$165) are popular attractions, and a excellent option for traveling to them is aboard the **Alaska Railroad** (round-trip about $100 adults/$50 children). **Museums** are inexpensive and informative. Many operate on a donation basis, while others charge nominal fees ($1–7).

C

CAR RENTAL

Renting a vehicle is the best way to see the sights of Alaska on your own schedule. Standard daily rates for cars in larger cities run from $40–$100 (or more), depending on size and style of vehicle. Weekly and weekend rates are available. If you are planning to drive from major cities to remote locations, check your rental company's policy on taking cars off paved roads. RV rentals are available in Anchorage, and offer a comfortable, flexible way to experience Alaska at your own pace. Peak-season rental of an intermediate size camper, however, may cost $1,500 a week, plus gas.

CHILDREN'S ACTIVITIES

Children can take part in almost any activity you choose. Among many inexpensive (or free) options are visits to local parks, hiking, fishing, sightseeing, and visiting wildlife centers *(see page 94)*.

CLIMATE

Summer in Alaska can be nothing short of glorious: seemingly end-less daylight with mild, invigorating temperatures. Some summers can be rainy, however, and travelers should come prepared. June is generally the driest month of summer, and has the most dramatic daylight hours. But Alaska's mosquitoes like June best, too, and snow (or mud) may still linger in the higher-elevation trails of Southcentral or in the far north of the Bush. You generally don't have to be concerned with lingering snow in Southeast during June, but be prepared for torrential rainfall any time of the year.

Winter temperatures are mild in Southeast, often above freezing. Frequent rains, however, can feel cold and raw. In many areas of Southeast, snow melts away quickly following winter storms. The communities of Prince William Sound, while technically a part of Southcentral, have all the moisture of Southeast's maritime climate, but with colder temperatures. The highest snow accumulation in the state occurs in these areas. The remainder of Southcentral, includ-ing Anchorage, the Kenai Peninsula and the Mat-Su Valley, has colder temperatures (generally below freezing), but more sun and less rain than communities to the south. Interior Alaska has still less rain and the most extreme temperatures: hot summers (occasionally in the 90s°F/30s°C) and frigid winters (down to –60°F/–50°C).

CLOTHING

Visitors should dress in layers. In summer, a T-shirt, topped by a sweatshirt or fleece and then a windbreaker will allow you to enjoy most outdoor activities. A lightweight, hooded rain jacket is also essential. If you're headed to the rainforests of Southeast, add rain pants and waterproof footwear to the list. Lightweight hat and gloves will be useful if you are going out on the water, even during summer. Winter travelers should bring a heavier, hooded, outer jacket, as well as warm socks, gloves, hats, and winter boots. One thing you won't need is a tie. Alaskans are known for their casual dress.

COMPLAINTS

It's always best if you address any complaints to the management of the company involved. If you are not satisfied with the results, you may file a complaint with the Better Business Bureau online at <www.thebbb.org> or by mail or in person at 3601 C Street, Suite 1378, Anchorage, AK 99503.

CRIME AND SAFETY

Alaska is not immune from the crime associated with other destinations. As always, common-sense guidelines will serve you well:
• Never hitchhike or pick up hitchhikers.
• Walking around towns or attractions during the day or early evening is generally safe, but avoid walking alone late at night around (or on) wooded, isolated trails – regardless of the deceptive amount of daylight. This is especially true for women.
• Do not carry large amounts of cash. Use traveler's checks or one of the many ATMs.
• Avoid wearing expensive jewelry.
• Leave your valuables in the hotel safe.
• To receive emergency help or to report a crime, dial 911.

CRUISING

Many visitors arrive in Alaska via cruise ship. This is a luxurious and exciting way to come to Alaska. Cruise ships sail through the spectacular Inside Passage arriving at Skagway, Ketchikan, Sitka, Juneau, and Misty Fjord in Southeast Alaska; some also continue on to the Southcentral communities of Valdez, Seward, Whittier, and Anchorage. More than a dozen cruise lines serve Alaska, with several small vessels offering excursions. Cruises start from Vancouver, BC, Los Angeles, San Francisco, and Seattle.

Cruise lines normally operate between May and September. They offer a variety of travel options including round-trip or one-way cruises, and cruises which are sold as part of a package tour. Such tours may also include air, rail, and/or motorcoach transportation within Alaska. Popular cruise lines serving Alaska include: Norwegian Cruise Line, Princess Cruises, Royal Caribbean Line, and Westours/Holland America Line.

Cruise Tours

Cruise-tours (a cruise plus a land extension) have become an increasingly popular way to see more of Alaska, particularly by those who have time and may only visit it once. This usually involves a cruise plus land stay in a hotel, or a cruise plus a train ride and hotel stay, all neatly arranged and packaged by the cruise lines, relieving passengers of all the headaches and organization.

Although the most popular cruises to Alaska are of seven days, extending your vacation by taking a cruise plus an escorted land tour can stretch to as many as 18 days, to include a cruise, plus the heart of Alaska, and the Canadian Rockies.

Alaska Cruise Trains

Specially constructed domed railcars are featured in the cruise-tour programs of the major cruise companies: Holland America Line-Westours, Princess Cruises, and Royal Caribbean International/ Celebrity Cruises. The domed cars (some are fitted with seats that can turn to allow passengers to face forwards or backwards) are fitted aboard trains operated by the Alaska Railroad, which is owned by the State of Alaska. The railway extends northwards, from Seward through Anchorage to Fairbanks, a distance of 470 miles (760km).

McKinley Explorer. Holland America Line-Westours has original 1950s domed railcars that have been specially converted for the company, aboard the McKinley Explorer. They were designed and built by the Budd Rail Company, and originally operated on the Sante Fe Railway. The railcars, each named after an Alaska river, are dubbed the Mercedez-Benz of the American rails. They are extremely smooth railcars, and run on six-wheel units (called 'trucks') instead of the usual four. The train has a full-service dining car.

Midnight Sun Express. Princess Cruises has had its own Midnight Sun Express train since 1984. It operates between Anchorage and Fairbanks. The upper level of the cars is completely glass-enclosed (Ultra Domes). The train has a full-service dining car.

Wilderness Express. The domed railcars on the Wilderness Express were specially constructed for Royal Caribbean International and Celebrity Cruises (owned by RCI) and feature full-length vista-domes. The train has a full-service dining car.

Shore Excursions

Shore excursions, too, have increased in number (and cost) over the years. They include flightseeing by floatplane or helicopter, salmon fishing, salmon bake, hiking, glacial ice treks, mountain biking, train rides, jeep safaris, and whale watching. One must-do excursion (if your cruise takes you to Skagway) is a trip on the White Pass & Yukon Route Railway.

Pre- and Post-Cruise Stays

The cruise lines have many combinations of pre- and post-cruise stays ashore to extend an Alaska vacation. Two of the major cruise lines, Holland America Line-Westours and Princess Cruises (both now owned by Carnival Corporation), have such comprehensive facilities ashore (hotels, tour buses, special glass-domed railcars) that they are committed to Alaska for many years. Holland America Line-Westours and Princess Tours (a division of Princess Cruises) have, between them, invested more than $300 million in Alaska. Indeed, Holland America Line-Westours is one of the state's largest private employers. Other cruise lines depend on what's left of the local transportation for their land tours. In 2001, for example, Holland America Line took 115,000 passengers to Alaska, while Princess Cruises took 180,000.

More Adventure

Those who are more adventurous (and have plenty of time) might want to consider one of the more unusual Alaska cruises to the far north, around the Pribilof Islands (these are known to be superb locations for bird-watching) and into the Bering Sea. These cruises are operated, on an infrequent basis, by the smaller, specialist expedition cruise companies.

CUSTOMS AND ENTRY REQUIREMENTS

If you are traveling to Alaska from abroad, bring a valid passport and the appropriate visa (unless you are a national of a country participating in the Visa Waiver Program). This new, all-inclusive requirement is the result of the Western Hemisphere Travel Initiative, which is being phased in from December 31, 2005 to December 2007. For complete and specific information on documentation requirements, contact your consulate or embassy, or go to the US State Department's website: <www.travel.state. gov>. A new procedure for all visitors entering the US is a two-digit finger scan and a digital photo, which will be taken at the port of entry. The process takes only a few seconds, and will be repeated upon departure.

US Customs allows you to bring personal effects, such as video cameras and fishing gear, without paying duties. If you are over 21, you may also bring in the following items duty-free: 1 liter of alcohol for personal use, 200 cigarettes (or 100 cigars – not from Cuba – or 3 pounds of smoking tobacco), and $100-worth of gifts. In order to claim these exemptions, you must plan to spend at least 72 hours in the US, and not have claimed these items within the preceding six months. Beyond those limits, expect to pay 3 percent on the first $1,000 (flat rate) of items for your personal use or for gifts. The flat rate can only be used once in 30 days. Most raw or plant material cannot be brought into the country without a special license. Foreign visitors may bring in up to $10,000 (US or foreign currency) with no required formalities. Larger sums must be declared when entering or leaving the country. For more information, contact the US Customs office at <www.customs.ustreas.gov>.

D

DRIVING

Renting a car in one of the larger cities and exploring other locations along the roadway is an excellent way to experience Alaska. Foreign drivers' licenses are generally valid in the US, but if they are not written in English you might consider getting an international license. Speed limits are usually 55mph (88km/h) on highways (a few are 65mph/104km/h), 45mph (72km/h) on major roads within city limits, 30mph (48km/h) in residential or business areas. School zones, identified by yellow signs, have a 20mph (32km/h) speed limit. Speeding infractions there, or on roads marked 'Construction Zone' are extremely costly in terms of potential danger and heavy fines.

In summer, drivers should keep their headlights on when traveling on highways, even in daytime. If five or more cars are lined up behind you, regardless of the speed you're traveling, Alaska law requires you to pull over at the first safe opportunity, and allow them to pass. Frustrated drivers attempting to pass a long line of RVs (and other vehicles) are frequent causes of serious or fatal highway accidents. If you are venturing outside of the larger cities, to more remote areas, be sure you have an adequate spare tire and a functional jack. Other good things to have on hand for remote travel are flares, an emergency medical kit, jumper cables, emergency rations, and a towrope. Don't count on conveniently spaced service stations (for gas or repairs). Try to keep your tank full. When traveling on unpaved roads, watch out for gravel hurled onto your windshield by passing trucks.

Winter driving in Alaska requires being prepared for the unexpected, including lengthy delays caused by accidents or avalanches. Again, keeping your tank full gives you more options (like heat) if you are stranded on the road. Heavy winter hats, gloves, and boots may be too cumbersome for wearing in the car, but throw them in the trunk, along with warm sleeping bags, a flashlight, matches, or lighter, an ice scraper, and all the summer emergency gear mentioned above. The Alaska Department of Transportation does an excellent job of plowing and sanding major roads following a storm, but it often takes a day or two. If a roadway is marked 'Closed' or 'Unmaintained,' don't go there. Studded snow tires are an excellent idea. If your rental car has an electrical cord tucked in the front grill or under the bumper, it leads to a handy head-bolt heater. When plugged in (and there are plugs everywhere, especially within the Interior), these heaters protect your car's engine from the frigid temperatures while parked for several hours or overnight.

No matter what the season, it's a good idea to find out about driving conditions and possible delays before beginning a road trip in Alaska. Current information is available by dialing 511, or at <http://511.alaska.gov>. For any emergency, dial 911, or (if out of range) dial 0 and ask the operator to connect you with emergency police, ambulance or fire services.

Alaska has strictly enforced drink-driving laws that involve mandatory prison sentences even for first-time offenders. Do not drink and drive.

E

ELECTRICITY

110 to 120 volts (60 cycle) AC is standard throughout the US. The plugs have two flat, parallel pins. Foreign visitors who don't have dual-voltage appliances will need a 110 volt transformer and an adaptor plug.

EMBASSIES AND CONSULATES

All embassies are located in Washington, DC (<www.embassy.org/embassies>). The only nation with a consulate in Alaska is Japan (3601 C Street, Suite 1300, Anchorage AK 99503).

EMERGENCIES (*see also* HEALTH & MEDICAL CARE *and* POLICE)

For all emergencies dial 911, or 0 if outside of 911 area.

G

GAY AND LESBIAN TRAVELERS

Anchorage, Fairbanks, and Juneau have active gay and lesbian populations. In Anchorage, Identity Inc. (<www.identityinc.org>) sponsors a statewide helpline, a newsletter, and the Gay and Lesbian Community Center (2110 E. Northern Lights, Suite A).

GETTING THERE

Airfare from Seattle to Anchorage can vary greatly, depending on season and how far in advance you buy tickets. Competing airlines sometimes offer tickets for as little as $200 round trip, but in general, expect to pay at least $300, with two-week advance purchase.

If you prefer to travel up by ferry, from Bellingham to Whittier, make sure it's not for reasons of economy. The trip aboard the Alaska Marine Highway System (<www.ferryalaska.com>) will take about six days of sailing, and will cost over $500 per adult for walk-ons. If you want to bring along a small vehicle (10ft/3m or less in length) add another $700. Larger vehicles and RVs cost considerably more. You may choose to sleep in sleeping bags rolled out in lounge areas, or to pitch a tent on the top deck, but if you want a stateroom, it will cost $175–800, depending on the location of cabin, number of berths, bathroom facilities, and whether you want linens provided.

Driving to Alaska from the Lower 48 (states) can be a more economical option, if your vehicle doesn't break down in some extremely remote location. The trip will take about a week, depending on driving style. Lodging, food, and current gas prices along the way are important considerations.

Most people choose to travel to Alaska on a cruise ship. There are many valid reasons for this choice: generally excellent lodging, food, and services, interesting land tours, and tour directors handling logistics. Cruises can even be economical, when you consider the costs of individual transportation, lodging, food, and tours for a week's stay in Alaska.

You cannot travel to Alaska by train; Alaska's railway system does not connect with Canada's, or with those of the Lower 48 United States.

GUIDES AND TOURS

Almost every city or town in Alaska offers a variety of organized tours (walking, helicopter, dogsled, kayak, flightseeing, wildlife, historical, and more). There are also guides and outfitters for hunting and fishing adventures. The best way to learn about guides and operators in the area you plan to visit is to contact the nearest Convention and Visitors Bureau *(see pages 122–4)*.

H

HEALTH CARE

Every major city in Alaska has its own hospital, and many of the smaller cities will have one as well, particularly if the city serves as a regional hub. The isolated communities of the Bush often have medical clinics, sometimes staffed by physicians' assistants rather than doctors.

Be sure to check your personal insurance provider or travel agent to be certain you are covered by health and accident insurance during your trip. Hospitals generally offer lists of medical providers for non-emergency medical needs. Your hotel may be able to provide a list of doctors, as well.

HOLIDAYS

The following is a list of national holidays (common to the whole of the United States) and Alaska state holidays. Banks, offices, post offices, and other state and federal agencies will probably be closed on these days:

January 1: New Year's Day
Third Monday in January: Martin Luther King Jr. Day
Third Monday in February: President's Day
Last Monday in March: Seward's Day
Last Monday in May: Memorial Day
July 4: Independence Day
First Monday in September: Labor Day
Second Monday in October: Columbus Day
October 18: Alaska Day
November 11: Veterans' Day
Fourth Thursday in November: Thanksgiving Day
December 25: Christmas Day

L

LOST PROPERTY

Each transportation system maintains its own lost and found property department:
Alaska Marine Highway System: tel: 800-642-0066.
Alaska Railroad: tel: 907-265-2494.
Anchorage's Ted Stevens International Airport:tel: 907-266-2623.
Fairbanks International Airport: tel:907-458-2530.
Juneau International: tel: 907-789-9539.

M

MEDIA

Radio and Television. Nearly all Alaska hotel rooms feature cable television. There are almost 100 radio stations located throughout the state.

Newspapers. The major newspapers in Alaska's three largest cities are the *Anchorage Daily News*, the *Fairbanks Daily News-Miner*, and the *Juneau Empire*. Nearly every community has its own local paper.

MONEY

The US dollar is made up of 100 cents. The coins are: 1 cent (penny), 5 cents (nickel), 10 cents (dime), and 25 cents (quarter). Common bank notes include $1, $5, $10, $20, $50, and $100, though local merchants are generally less than thrilled to be offered a note of any denomination over $20, unless you are making an expensive purchase.

Credit, Charge, and Debit Cards. Most major credit, charge, and debit cards are readily accepted at nearly all places of business. ATM machines are located in all but the very smallest villages.

Currency Exchange. You should obtain US dollars before leaving home or get cash from one of the many ATM machines throughout the state. There are no foreign-currency exchange bureaus in Alaska. The Wells Fargo Bank branch located in the 5th Avenue Mall (in Anchorage) has the only currency exchange desk in the state.

Sales Tax. There is no state sales tax in Alaska. Local governments, however, often do have a sales tax and a bed tax on accommodations.

Traveler's Checks. Traveler's checks are accepted by most places of business. It's best to have them denominated in US dollars.

N

NATIONAL PARKS

Information about the major national parks can be obtained from the following addresses.

Bering Land Bridge National Preserve (National Park Service, PO Box 1029, Kotzebue 99752, <www.nps.gov/bela>).

Cape Krusenstern National Monument (National Park Service, PO Box 1029, Kotzebue 99752, <www.nps.gov/cakr>).

Denali National Park and Preserve (National Park Service, PO Box 9, Denali Park 99755, <www.nps.gov/dena>).

Gates of the Arctic National Park and Preserve (National Park Service, 201 First Ave, Fairbanks 99701, <www.nps.gov/gaar>).

Glacier Bay National Park and Preserve (National Park Service, PO Box 140, Gustavus 99826-0141, <www.nps.gov/glba>).

Katmai National Park and Preserve (National Park Service, PO Box 7, King Salmon 99613, <www.nps.gov/katm>).

Kenai Fjords National Park (National Park Service, PO Box 1727, Seward 99664, <www.nps.gov/kefj>).

Klondike Gold Rush National Historical Park (National Park Service, PO Box 517, Skagway 99840, <www.nps.gov/klgo>).

Lake Clark National Park and Preserve (National Park Service, 4230 University Dve, Suite 311, Anchorage 99508, <www.nps.gov/lacl>).

Noatak National Preserve (National Park Service, PO Box 1029, Kotzebue 99752, <www.nps.gov/noat>).

Sitka National Historical Park (National Park Service, 103 Monastery Street, Sitka 99835, <www.nps.gov/sitk>).

Wrangell-St. Elias National Park and Preserve (National Park Service, PO Box 439, Copper Center 99573-0439, <www.nps.gov/wrst>).

Yukon-Charley Rivers National Preserve (National Park Service, PO Box 167, Eagle 99738, <www.nps.gov/yuch>).

OPENING HOURS

Banks. Larger cities generally have at least one branch open every day of the week, Mon–Sat 9am–7pm, Sun noon–4pm, but hours may vary depending upon the bank's location.

Offices. Basically 9am–5pm (give or take a half hour).

Post offices. Generally Mon–Fri 10am–5pm. Many open earlier and/ or remain open later. Saturday hours are usually morning or afternoon only. The Anchorage airport post office is always open.

Stores. At the very least Mon–Fri 10am–6pm; Many malls and discount stores are open until 9 or 10pm. Grocery stores in larger cities are open until late at night. In Anchorage, some are open 24 hours.

Restaurants. Most restaurants open for breakfast, lunch and dinner, usually closing by 10pm on weekdays and later on weekends.

P

POLICE

In any emergency, dial 911, or if out of 911 range, dial 0. Public safety in Alaska is provided by local village public safety officers (in remote villages), city police and Alaska State Troopers.

POST OFFICES

A domestic letter costs 37 cents to mail, a domestic postcard 23 cents; a postcard sent overseas costs 70 cents. Stamps can be bought at post offices, grocery stores, and at some hotel reception desks. Mailboxes are painted blue, and located throughout the cities and communities of Alaska.

PUBLIC TRANSPORTATION

For airport transfers, *see page 104*. For information on transporation within cities and towns, see BUDGETING FOR YOUR TRIP, *page 105*.

Alaska Marine Highway System. An enjoyable and flexible mode for visiting communities in Southeast, Southcentral, and (seasonally) southwest Alaska is aboard one of the eight ferries of the Alaska

Marine Highway System. As well as vehicles, bicycles, kayaks, and inflatables may, for a fee, be taken onto the ferry. You can find out about individual vessels, research routes and schedules, and make reservations online at <www.ferryalaska.com>.

T

TELEPHONE/FAX

Telephones. Directory (dial 411) or operator (dial 0) assistance may be dialed free of charge from any pay phone in Alaska. Telephone numbers beginning with 800, 888, 866 or 877 are toll-free. In order to place a domestic, long-distance call within the US (or to Canada), dial 1 + the area code + the seven-digit number. For international calls (other than to Canada) dial 011 + country code + city code + number. For collect, operator-assisted or person-to-person calls dial 0 + area code + number, then specify to the operator which type of call you are making. Ask for the overseas operator if it's an international call.

All of Alaska is covered by area code 907. If you a dialing from one Alaska city to another, you'll generally need to dial 1 + 907 + the seven-digit number. The charge for a local pay-phone call is 25 cents. US pay phones do not accept pennies. Probably the least expensive way to make long-distance calls is to buy a pre-paid, long-distance calling card. These are available at convenience, grocery, discount, and giant warehouse stores. If you bring a calling card with you, check with the provider that it will work in Alaska.

Hotels often add a hefty surcharge to local or long-distance calls, even those placed on a calling card. Your best and cheapest bet is to use a public pay phone with your prepaid card.

Cell phone coverage is good within Alaska's major population areas and along some paved highways. Do not count on coverage in outlying areas. Check with your wireless provider in advance to find out if your cell phone works in Alaska, and what roaming fees you will be charged (they can be staggering).

If you want to be sure that you can be in telephone contact at all times, renting a satellite phone is your best bet.

Fax. You can send a fax (expensively) from most hotels in Alaska, or (less expensively) from The UPS Store, Mailboxes Etc., or Kinko's outlets, located in major Alaska cities.

TIME ZONES

Almost the entire state of Alaska lies within the Alaska time zone, which is one hour earlier than Pacific time, and four hours earlier than Eastern time. Like much of the rest of the US, daylight savings time is in effect from 2am on the first Sunday in April (turn clocks ahead one hour, or 'spring forward') until 2am on the last Sunday in October ('fall back' one hour).

TIPPING

Gratuities are never included in restaurant prices but are definitely expected by the person serving you. In some cases, however, especially with large groups, a gratuity has been included when you get the bill. Be sure to check before paying. You can indicate your level of satisfaction with the service by the amount of tip you leave, but if you leave no tip, it will look like ignorance (or meanness) on your part.

In restaurants, bars, and nightclubs, the customary tip is 15–20 percent of the bill. A tip is not expected at cafeteria-style or fast-food restaurants where you order food at the counter. Tip bartenders 10–15 percent; give porters $1 per bag, valet parking attendants $1 per car, checkroom attendants $1 per garment, and hotel housekeepers $1–2 per day. Taxi drivers expect a tip of around 15 percent of the fare. Barbers or hairstylists usually get a 15–20 percent tip. If you find a service station where attendants actually pump your gas (most stations are self-service), you don't need to tip them.

TOILETS

Public toilets in Alaska's cities are found in hotel lobbies or in restaurants, coffee shops, and bars (they prefer – and some require – that you be a paying customer). Other options include museums, department stores, shopping malls, railway or bus stations, and service stations. When you travel along the road system, away from cities, the options become more primitive (outhouses or chemical toilets) and are spaced further apart (usually found at campgrounds or picnic areas).

TOURIST INFORMATION

Alaska Public Lands Information Centers: 605 W. Fourth Ave, Suite 105, Anchorage 99501, tel: 907-271-2737; PO Box 359, Tok 99780, tel: 907-883-5667; 250 Cushman Street, Suite 1A, Fairbanks 99701, tel: 907-456-0527; 50 Main Street, Ketchikan 99901, tel: 907-228-6220.

Alaska Travel Industry Association: 2600 Cordova Street, Suite 201, Anchorage 99503, <www.travelalaska.com>.

Anchorage (Girdwood and **Portage)**: Anchorage Convention and Visitors Bureau, 524 W. Fourth Ave, Anchorage 99501-2122, tel: 907-276-4118, fax: 907-278-5559, <www.anchorage.net>.

Barrow: City of Barrow, PO Box 629, Barrow 99723, tel: 907-852-5211, fax: 907-852-5871.

Bethel: Bethel Chamber, PO Box 329, Bethel 99559, tel: 907-543-2911, fax: 907-543-2255, <www.bethelakchamber.org>.

Cordova: Cordova Chamber, PO Box 99, Cordova 99574, tel: 907-424-7260, fax: 907-424-7259, <www.cordovachamber.com>.

Denali (National Park and Preserve): National Park Service, PO Box 9, Denali Park 99755l, <www.nps.gov/dena>.

Dillingham: Dillingham Chamber, PO Box 348, Dillingham 99576, tel: 907-842-5115, fax: 907-842-4097, <www.dillinghamak.com>.

Fairbanks: Fairbanks Convention and Visitors Bureau, 550 First Ave, Fairbanks 99701-4790, tel: 907-465-5774 or 800-327-5774, fax: 907-452-4190, <www.explorefairbanks.com>.

Gustavus: Gustavus Visitors Association, PO Box 167, Gustavus 99826; no phone, <www.gustavusalaska.org>.

Haines:: Haines Convention and Visitors Bureau, PO Box 530, Haines 99827, tel: 907-766-2234, fax: 907-766-3155, <www.haines.ak.us>.

Homer (Seldovia): Homer Chamber, PO Box 541, Homer 99603, tel: 907-235-7740, fax: 907-235-8766, <www.homeralaska.org>.

Juneau: Juneau Convention and Visitors Bureau, One Sealaska Plaza, Suite 305, Juneau 99801, tel: 888-581-2201 or 907-586-2201, fax: 907-586-6304, <www.traveljuneau.com>.

Kenai: Kenai Convention and Visitors Bureau, 11471 Kenai Spur Highway, Kenai 99611, tel: 907-283-1991, fax: 907-283-2230, <www.visitkenai.com>.

Ketchikan: Ketchikan Visitors Bureau, 131 Front Street, Ketchikan 99901, tel: 800-770-3300 or 907-225-6166, fax: 907-225-4250, <www.visit-ketchikan.com>.

King Salmon: *(see Alaska Travel Industry Association)*.

Kodiak: Kodiak Island Convention and Visitors Bureau, 100 Marine Way, Suite 200, Kodiak 99615, tel: 907-486-4782 or 800-789-4782, fax: 907-486-6545, <www.kodiak.org>.

Kotzebue: City of Kotzebue, PO Box 46, Kotzebue 99752, tel: 907-442-3401, <www.cityofkotzebue.com>.

Nome: Nome Convention and Visitors Bureau, PO Box 240 H-P, Nome 99762, tel: 907-443-6624, fax: 907-443-5832, <www.nomealaska.org>.

Palmer, Wasilla, Talkeetna: Mat-Su Convention and Visitors Bureau, HC 01 Box 6166 J21, Palmer 99645, tel: 907-746-5000, fax: 907-746-2698, <www.alaskavisit.com>.

Petersburg: Petersburg Visitor Information, PO Box 649, Petersburg 99833, tel: 907-772-4636 or 866-484-4700, fax: 907-772-3646, <www.petersburg.org>.

Seward: Seward Visitor Information Cache, PO Box 749, Seward 99664, tel: 907-224-8051, <www.seward.com>.

Sitka: Sitka Convention and Visitors Bureau, PO Box 1226, Sitka 99835, tel: 907-747-5940, fax: 907-747-3739, <www.sitka.org>.

Skagway: Skagway Convention and Visitors Bureau, PO Box 1029, Skagway 99840, tel: 907-983-2854, fax: 907-983-3854, <www.skagway.org>.

Soldotna: Soldotna Chamber, 44790 Sterling Hwy, Soldotna 99669, tel: 907-262-9814, fax: 907-262-3566, <www.soldotnachamber.com>.

Talkeetna: *(see Palmer)*.

Unalaska/Dutch Harbor: Unalaska/Port of Dutch Harbor Convention and Visitors Bureau, PO Box 545, Unalaska 99685, tel: 877-581-2612 or 907-581-2612, fax: 907-581-2613, <www.unalaska.info>.

Valdez: Valdez Convention and Visitors Bureau, PO Box 1603, Valdez 99686, tel: 800-770-5954 or 907-835-2984, fax: 907-835-4845, <www.valdezalaska.org>.

Wasilla: *(see Palmer)*.

Whittier: Whittier Visitors Center, PO Box 608, Whittier 99693, tel: 907-472-2327, fax: 907-472-2404, <www.ci.whittier.ak. us>.

Wrangell: Wrangell Chamber, PO Box 49, Wrangell 99929, tel: 907-874-3901, fax: 907-874-3905, <www.wrangellchamber.org>.

Yakutat: City and Borough of Yakutat, PO Box 160, Yakutat 99684, tel: 907-784-3323, fax: 907-784-3281, <www.travelalaska.com>.

TRAVELERS WITH DISABILITIES

Almost every hotel in Alaska can accommodate people with disabilities, and frequently they are offered the best room in the house. In smaller communities, advance discussion may be needed concerning the specifics of accessibility. Many recreational opportunities are available to travelers with disabilities. Challenge Alaska (3350 Commercial Drive, Suite 208, Anchorage 99501, tel: 907-344-7399, <www.challenge.ak.org>) offers a creative variety of options, including adaptive skiing in winter and sea kayaking in summer.

The Alaska Marine Highway System offers discounts on certain routes for passengers with disabilities. It helps if you can give advance notice, so that ferry personnel or day-cruise tour operators are able to accommodate special needs. However, all vessels in Alaska fall under United States Coast Guard regulations, and therefore do not have to meet the requirements of the Americans with Disabilities Act (ADA) .

W

WEBSITES

Additional websites that may be useful in planning an Alaska vacation include:

Alaska Department of Fish and Game: <www.adfg.state.ak.us>; hunting and fishing information, licensing.

Alaska Marine Highway System: <www.ferryalaska.com>; schedules, fares, descriptions of services.

Alaska Public Lands Information Centers: <www.nps.gov/aplic>; inter-agency information on all recreational land use opportunities on Alaska's public lands.

Alaska Railroad: <www.akrr.com>; schedules, fares; rail-tour packages.

Alaska Wilderness Recreation and Tourism Association: <www.awrta.org>; comprehensive list of eco-tourism operators, guides and lodges.

Anchorage Daily News **visitor information**:: <www.alaska.com>; huge variety of interesting information for visitors, sponsored by Alaska's largest newspaper.

Geophysical Institute of Alaska Fairbanks: <www.gi.alaska.edu>; fascinating earth science information on Alaska, including aurora borealis predictions, volcano watches, and earthquake or tsunami updates.

WEIGHTS AND MEASURES

The imperial system is used in Alaska, as in the rest of the USA.

Recommended Hotels

Lodging in Alaska's major cities ranges from uniquely Alaska-styled luxury hotels to small, privately owned B&Bs and hostels. National chain hotels abound in many of the larger cities. Prices throughout Alaska vary greatly and may not be an accurate indication of relative quality. The prices below reflect peak-season rates for double occupancy, and do not include bed tax, sales tax or gratuities *(see Tipping, page 121)*. This is by no means a complete list of all Alaska hotels, but rather a sampling of lodging options in various cities across the state. Check with the closest Convention and Visitors Bureau for all hotels nearest your destination *(see Tourist Information, pages 122–4).*

$$$$	$250 or more
$$$	$200–249
$$	$125–199
$	$124 or less

SOUTHEAST

KETCHIKAN

The Gilmore Hotel $ *326 Front Street, 99901, tel: 907-25-9423 or 800-275-9423, fax: 907-225-7442, <www.gilmorehotel.com/index. htm>.* Overlooking the waterfront and listed on the National Register of Historic Places. Family plan available. Restaurant. 38 rooms.

The Narrows Inn $ *4871 N. Tongass Hwy, 99901, tel: 907-247-2600 or 888-686-2600, fax: 907-247-2602, <www.narrowsinn.com/index. html>.* Watch the boat and seaplane activity on the Tongass Narrows from the private balconies of the ocean-view rooms. Complimentary breakfast. Children under 12 free. Restaurant. 47 rooms.

The New York Hotel $ *207 Stedman Street, 99901, tel: 907-225-0246 or 866-225-0246, fax: 907-225-1803, <www.thenewyorkhotel.*

com>. Small downtown hotel on the National Register of Historic Places, updated to include modern amenities while retaining the charm of a small inn. Non-smoking. Restaurant. 12 rooms.

West Coast Cape Fox Lodge $$ *800 Venetia Way, 99901, tel: 907-225-8001 or 866-225-8001, fax: 907-225-8286, <www. capefoxcorp.com/cflodge1.html>*. A beautiful hotel situated in the Tongass National Forest, just a tram ride away from downtown. Totem carvings and other Native Alaskan art complement the natural setting. Restaurant. 74 rooms.

JUNEAU

Alaskan Hotel & Bar $ *167 S. Franklin Street, 99801, tel: 907-586 1000 or 800-327-9347, fax: 907-463-3775*. Landmark hotel refurbished with oak and stained glass. Family rooms. Under-12s free. Restaurant. 44 rooms.

Goldbelt Hotel $$ *51 Egan Drive, 99801, tel: 907-586-6900 or 888-478-6909, fax: 907-463-5861, <www.goldbelthotel.com>*. Extensive collection of Tlingit art on display. Restaurant. 105 rooms.

Prospector Hotel $$ *375 Whittier Street, 99801, tel: 907-586-3737 or 800-331-2711, fax: 907-586-1204, <www.prospectorhotel. com>*. Newly remodeled large suites and rooms overlook Gastineau Channel and Douglas Island. Restaurant. 62 rooms.

Westmark Baranof Hotel $$ *127 N. Franklin Street, 99801, tel: 907-586-2660 or 800-544-0970, fax: 907-586-8315, <www.west markhotels.com>*. Historic hotel recently restored to original art-deco style. A favorite of visiting Alaskans. Restaurants. 196 rooms.

SOUTHCENTRAL

ANCHORAGE

Alyeska Prince $$$$ *1000 Arlberg Avenue, Girdwood, tel: 907-754-1111 or 800-880-3880, fax: 907-754-2200; email: reservations@*

alyeskaresort.com, <*www.alyeskaresort.com*>. Skiing draws visitors to this hotel 37 miles (60km) south of Anchorage at the Alyeska Ski Resort. Rooms range from average to elegant. Enjoy the pool, sauna, Japanese cuisine, and various tour packages.

Anchorage Grand Hotel $$ *505 W. 2nd Avenue, 99501, tel: 907-929-8888 or 888-800-0640, fax: 907-929-8899, <www.anchorage grandhotel.com/http>*. All-suite hotel close to downtown activities and within walking distance of the station. Rooms have two separate sleeping areas and complete kitchen facilities, making this a comfortable stop for families. Continental breakfast. 31 rooms.

Anchorage Hotel $$$ *330 E Street, 99501, tel: 907-272-4553 or 800-544-0988, fax: 907-277-4483, <www.historicanchoragehotel. com>*. Attractively renovated historic downtown hotel. Intimate lobby with fireplace; 26 spacious rooms. Breakfast buffet included. Street-side rooms can be noisy. Additional charge for parking.

Aspen Hotel $$ *108 E. 8th Avenue, 99501, tel: 907-868-1605, fax: 907-868-3520, <www.aspenhotelsak.com>*. Pleasant, well-planned facilities. High-ceilinged rooms with mini-refrigerators and microwaves; family suites with bunk beds and PlayStations. Within walking distance of most downtown activities. Continental breakfast. Limited on-site parking. 89 rooms.

Comfort Inn Ship Creek $$ *111 Ship Creek Avenue, 99501, tel: 907-277-6887 or 800-362-6887, fax: 907-274-9830, <www. choicehotels.com>*. Fish for salmon in the creek behind this newer hotel close to downtown; they'll even loan you a fishing pole. Large comfortable rooms; within walking distance of the city center and the railroad station. Continental breakfast. 100 rooms.

Hotel Captain Cook $$$$ *4th & K Street, 99501, tel: 907-276-6000 or 800-843-1950, fax: 907-343-2298, <www.captaincook. com>*. Alaska's premier locally owned hotel. Most rooms have wonderful views of the mountains or Cook Inlet. Helpful staff. Rooms are stylish and well-maintained. Additional charge for parking. Three restaurants, three bars, health club. 547 rooms.

Inlet Tower $$ *1200 L Street, 99501, tel: 907-276-0110 or 800-544-0786, fax: 907-258-4914, <www.inlettower.com/>*. Magnificent views of Cook Inlet and the Chugach Mountains. In a residential area near the city center. Spacious rooms with microwaves; exceptional service. Restaurant. Free parking. 180 rooms.

Lakeshore Motor Inn $$ *3009 Lakeshore Drive, 99517, tel: 907-248-3485 or 800-770-3000, fax: 907-248-1544, <www.lakeshore motorinn.com>*. Conveniently near Lake Hood for those planning fly-in hunting or fishing trips; plenty of freezer space for your catch. This quiet, affordably priced hotel has a beautiful garden where guests can relax after a day of sightseeing. 44 rooms.

Long House Alaskan Hotel $$ *4335 Wisconsin Street, tel: 907-243-2133 or 888-243-2133, <www.longhousehotel.com>*. Near the airport and Lake Hood, this economical small hotel is a practical choice for anyone planning fly-in fishing trips. Walk-in freezer to store your catch. Large rooms. Continental breakfast.

Puffin Inn Hotel $$ *4400 Spenard Road, 99517, tel: 907-243-4044 or 800-478-3346, <www.puffininn.net>*. Rooms are graded from deluxe to economy depending on size and amenities. Boutique rooms are in a separate nearby location. Convenient to airport. Freezer space available for your catch. Continental breakfast. 186 rooms.

Sheraton Hotel $$$ *401 E. 6th Avenue, 99501, tel: 907-276-8700 or 800-478-8700, fax: 907-276-7561, <www.sheratonanchoragehotel. com>*. The jade-tiled staircase sets an elegant tone for this centrally located hotel, within walking distance of the city center. Generous sized rooms. Restaurants. Free parking. 371 rooms.

Spenard Motel $ *3960 Spenard Road, 99517, tel: 907-243-6917, fax: 907-248-4614, <email: spenardjaejean@hotmail.com>*. A clean, comfortable, budget motel. Convenient for the airport and Lake Hood.

Voyager Hotel $$ *501 K Street, 99501, tel: 907-277-9501 or 800-247-9070, fax: 907-274-0333, <www.voyagerhotel.com>*. Downtown location close to restaurants and entertainment. Large, airy, comfortable rooms are all mini-suites with kitchens. Continental breakfast. Non-smoking. Extra charge for parking. 40 rooms.

TALKEETNA

Talkeetna Alaskan Lodge $$$ *Mile 12.5 Talkeetna Spur Road, tel: 907-265-4501 or 888-959-9590, fax 907-263-5559, <www.talkeetna lodge.com>.* A striking multi-story lobby offers memorable views of Mount McKinley and Denali National Park. Alaska Native artwork in rooms and public areas. Restaurants. 200 rooms.

KENAI PENINSULA

SOLDOTNA

Best Western King Salmon Motel $$ *35546A Kenai Spur Hwy, 99669, tel: 907-262-5857 or 888-262-5857, fax: 907-262-9441, <www.bestwestern.com>.* Convenient for Kenai River fishing. Children under 12 free. Restaurant. 49 rooms.

Kenai River Lodge $$ *393 West Riverside Drive, 99669, tel: 907-262-2492, fax: 907-262-7332, <www.kenairiverlodge.com>.* Family-run. Guests can cast for salmon at Kenai River frontage; all rooms have river views. Continental breakfast. 25 rooms.

HOMER

Beluga Lake Lodge $ *204 Ocean Drive Loop, 99603, tel: 907-235-5995, fax: 907-235-2640, <www.belugalakelodge.com>.* Overlooking Kachemak Bay, this small lodge is situated between downtown Homer and the Homer Spit. Restaurant. 32 rooms.

Land's End Resort $$ *4786 Homer Spit Road, 99603, tel: 907-235-0400 or 800-478-0400, fax: 907-234-0420, <www.lands-end-resort.com>.* Near the boat harbor and convenient for fishing charters, this waterfront hotel offers views of Kachemak Bay and the Kenai Mountains. Restaurant. 80 rooms.

Ocean Shores Motel $$ *451 Sterling Hwy, 99603, tel: 90-235-7775 or 800-770-7775, fax: 907-235-8639, <www.oceanshores alaska.com>.* On the outskirts of Homer above a private beach, this quiet location is in walking distance of most attractions. 32 rooms.

SEWARD

Harborview Inn $$ *804 Third Avenue, PO Box 1305, 99664, tel: 907-224-3217 or 888-324-3217, fax: 907-224-3218, <www. sewardhotel.com>.* Within walking distance of downtown and the small boat harbor. 37 rooms.

Seward Windsong Lodge $$ *½ mile Exit Glacier/Herman Leirer Rd, 99664, tel: 877-777-2805 or 777-2805 (in Anchorage), <www. sewardwindsong.com>.* In a beautiful glacial valley just outside Seward, this warm, rustic lodge complex is surrounded by spruce trees. Shuttle service to Seward. Restaurant. May–Sept. 108 rooms.

Van Gilder Hotel $$ *308 Adams Street, 99664, tel: 907-224-3079 or 800-204-6835, fax: 907-224-3689, <www.vangilderhotel. com>.* Historic hotel that reflects a bygone era while incorporating basic modern amenities. Downtown and close to most major activities. 24 rooms.

KODIAK

Best Western Kodiak Inn $$ *236 Rezanof Drive West, 99615, tel: 907-486-5712 or 888-563-4254, fax: 907-486-3430, <www. kodiakinn.com>.* Tucked into the side of Pillar Mountain with views of downtown Kodiak and the harbors. Rooms in the main building have been renovated. Public hot tub. Continental breakfast. Fine dining restaurant. 80 rooms.

Buskin River Inn $$ *1395 Airport Way, 99615, tel: 907-487-2700 or 800-544-2202, fax: 907-487-4447, <www.kodiakadventure. com>.* A tranquil wooded setting outside of town where eagles, deer, and foxes are frequent visitors. Freezer available for game and fish. Restaurant. 50 rooms.

Russian Heritage Inn $ *119 Yukon Street, 99615, tel: 907-486-5657, fax: 907-486-4643, <www.geocities.com/russianheritageinn>.* Quiet location with simple, somewhat small rooms. 25 rooms.

PRINCE WILLIAM SOUND

CORDOVA

Orca Adventure Lodge $$ *2500 Orca Road, 99574, tel: 907-424-7249 or 866-424-6722, <www.orcaadventurelodge.com>.* On Orca Bay 3 miles (5km) from town, an old cannery converted into an attractive hotel with full amenities. No phones or TV. 27 rooms.

Prince William Motel $ *510 2nd Street, 99574, tel: 907-424-3201, fax: 907-424-2260; email: <pwmotel@yahoo.com>.* Good central motel. Under-11s free in parents' room. 16 rooms.

VALDEZ

Aspen Hotel $$ *100 Meals Avenue, 99686, tel: 907-835-4445 or 800-483-7848, fax: 907-835-2437, <www.aspenhotelsak.com>.* Large, comfortable rooms. Continental breakfast. 104 rooms.

Best Western Valdez Harbor Inn $$ *100 N. Harbor Drive, 99686, tel: 907-835-3434 or 888-222-3440, fax: 907-835-2308, <www.valdezharborinn.com>.* On the harbor, this newly remodeled hotel offers a central location for tour boats and sightseeing. Children 12 and under free. Restaurant. 88 rooms.

INTERIOR

DENALI PARK

Denali Bluffs Hotel $$$ *Mile 238.3 George Parks Hwy, 99755, tel: 907-683-7000 or 866-683-8500, <www.denalialaska.com>.* This hotel consists of a series of low-rise buildings overlooking Denali Park. Under-12s free in parents' room. Restaurant. Mid-May–mid-Sept. 112 rooms.

Denali Park Hotel $ *Mile 247 George Parks Hwy, 99743, tel: 907-683-1800 or 866-683-1800; email: <stay@denaliparkhotel.com>, <denaliparkhotel.com>.* Small hotel with clean, comfortable rooms in a beautiful setting. Vintage Alaska Railroad cars house the hotel lobby and restaurant. Mid-May–mid-Sept. 42 rooms.

Denali Princess Wilderness Lodge $$$ *Mile 238.5 George Parks Hwy, 99755, tel: 907-683-2282 or 800-426-0500, fax: 907-683-2545, <www.princesslodges.com>.* Large complex in dramatic natural setting; accommodation in pleasant log buildings. Restaurants. Mid-May–mid-Sept. 440 rooms.

McKinley Village Lodge $$$ *Mile 231 George Parks Hwy, 99755, tel: 907-683-8900 or 800-276-7234, fax: 907-258-3668, <www.denaliparkresorts.com>.* A lodge-style hotel with nature path and park trails nearby. Restaurant. Mid-May–mid-Sept. 150 rooms.

FAIRBANKS

The Bridgewater $$ *723 1st Avenue, 99701, tel: 907-452-6661 or 800-528-4916, fax: 907-452-6126, <www.fountainheadhotels.com>.* This small, downtown hotel has the intimate feel of a bed-and-breakfast while providing standard hotel services. Bathrooms have showers only, no tubs. Closed mid-May–mid-Sept. 94 rooms.

Chena Hotsprings Resort Summer **$**, winter **$$** *Mile 56.5 Chena Hot Springs Rd, 99711, tel: 907-451-8104 or 800-478-4681, fax: 907-451-8151, <www.chenahotsprings.com>.* An hour's drive from Fairbanks, this hotel is part of a resort that grew up around the mineral springs. Peak season is winter when sightings of the aurora borealis are common. Basic but clean rooms. Restaurant. 90 rooms.

Fairbanks Princess Riverside Lodge $$$ *4477 Pikes Landing Road, tel: 907-455-4477 or 800-426-0500, fax: 907-455-4476, <www.princessalaskalodges.com>.* Near the airport along the Chena River, this hotel offers a spacious outdoor deck for dining, or watching activities along the river. Rooms are clean and adequate. Restaurant features buffet-style lunches and fine dining in the evening. 325 rooms.

Marriott Spring Hill Suites $$ *575 1st Avenue, 99701, tel: 907-451-6552 or 877-729-0197, fax: 907-451-6553, <www.springhill suites.com>.* On the Chena River, these suites are comfortable for an extended stay. Popular with business travelers because of the complimentary high-speed Internet in every room. Continental breakfast. Fine dining; extensive wine list. 140 rooms.

Pike's Waterfront Lodge $$$ *1850 Hoselton Road, 99709, tel: 907-456-4500 or 877-774-2400, fax 907-456-4515, <www.pikes lodge.com>.* On the Chena River near the airport. Rustic lodge-style décor, large rooms (some with Jacuzzis), exercise room, wireless Internet in lobby only. Continental breakfast.

River's Edge Resort $$ *4200 Boat Street, 99709, tel: 907-474-0286 or 800-770-3343, fax: 907-474-3665, <www.riversedge.net>.* Family-friendly hotel in landscaped grounds by the quiet Chena River; 86 cottages and 8 rooms in main building. Restaurant.

THE BUSH

BARROW

King Eider Inn $$ *1752 Ahkovak Street, 99723, tel: 907-852-4700 or 888-303-4337, fax: 907-852-2025, <www.kingeider.net>.* Barrow's newest hotel has Native artwork in the lobby. Non-smoking. 19 rooms.

Top of the World Hotel $$ *1200 Agvik Street, 99723, tel: 907-852-3900, 800-882-8478 or 800-478-8520 (in-state), <www. topoftheworldhotel.com>.* The oceanside rooms have great Arctic Ocean views. Restaurant adjacent. 43 rooms.

NOME

Nome Nugget Inn $$–$$$ *Front Street and Bering Avenue, 99762, tel: 907-443-4189 or 877-443-2323, fax: 907-443-5966, <www.nomenuggetinn.com>.* A taste of frontier life at the finish line of the Iditarod. Restaurant. 47 rooms.

Recommended Restaurants

Dining in Alaska is not cheap, but the range and quality of restaurants rival that of similar-sized communities in the Lower 48 states. The following list represents a sampling of what you might expect in selected cities across Alaska. The prices listed are typical for a dinner for one, without alcohol. This list is by no means exhaustive. Check with the local Convention and Visitors Bureau for a complete listing *(see Tourist Information, pages 122–4)*.

$$$$	$30 and over
$$$	$20–29
$$	$10–19
$	$10 or less

SOUTHEAST

KETCHIKAN

Bar Harbor Restaurant $$$ *2813 Tongass Avenue, tel: 907-225-2813*. Lunch and dinner Mon–Sat (summer), Tues–Sat (winter). Dining room overlooks Tongass Narrows and there's a back deck. Burritos, pasta, seafood, beer, wine. Reservations recommended.

Burger Queen $$ *518 Water Street, tel: 907-225-6060*. Mon–Sat lunch and early dinner (summer), Mon–Tues lunch (winter). For fast food with an Alaskan twist, try their fried halibut sandwich. Hamburgers, fries, and a variety of salads also available.

Diaz Café $$ *335 Stedman Street, tel: 907-225-2257*. Lunch and dinner Tues–Sun. Immaculate family-owned diner with a mix of Filipino, American, and Chinese fare. Try their chicken adobo.

Heen Kahidi Restaurant $$$$ *800 Venetia Avenue, tel: 907-225-8001*. Breakfast, lunch, and dinner daily. Open beams, and outstanding views from the huge windows. Extensive menu emphasizes local seafood specialties. Bar. Reservations recommended.

Ocean View Restorante $$ *1831 Tongass Avenue, tel: 907-225-7566.* Daily lunch and dinner. Local favorite that features Mexican and Italian fare. Beer and wine. Reservations recommended.

JUNEAU

BaCar's $$ *230 Seward Street, 99801, tel: 907-463-4202.* Breakfast and lunch daily. Great breakfasts, fresh bread, and home-cooked food have earned BaCar's a solid reputation among local people.

Di Sopra $$$$ *429 W. Willoughby Avenue, 99801, tel: 907-586-3150.* Dinner daily (summer), Tues–Sat (winter). Traditional Italian menu utilizes Alaskan seafood in dishes like *tuto mare Alaska*.

Fiddlehead Restaurant $$ *429 W. Willoughby Avenue, 99801, tel: 907-586-3150.* Breakfast, lunch, dinner daily. Family-friendly restaurant features many vegetarian dishes. Alaskan halibut burger and fisherman's pie typify their creative use of locally sourced ingredients.

The Gold Room $$$$ *127 N. Franklin Street, 99801, tel: 907-463-6222.* Dinner daily. Top-rated menu and sophisticated décor with an original art-deco skylight. Bar.

Hangar on the Wharf $$ *Suite 5 Fisherman's Wharf, 99801, tel: 907-586-5081.* Lunch and dinner daily. Watch floatplanes land outside. Simple lunch menu features soups and salads; dinner menu offers jambalaya and seafood specialties such as halibut tacos.

SOUTHCENTRAL

ANCHORAGE

Arctic Roadrunner $ *2477 Arctic Boulevard, tel: 907-279-7311,* and *5300 Old Seward Hwy, tel: 907-561-1245.* Lunch and dinner

Mon–Sat. Popular places for a fast meal that doesn't taste like fast food. Alaska-themed burgers and sandwiches. No credit cards.

Corsair $$$$ *944 W. 5th Avenue, 99501, tel: 907-278-4502.* Dinner Mon–Sat. A well-deserved reputation for memorable European cuisine in an intimate atmosphere. Bar. Reservations recommended.

Crow's Nest $$$$ *939 W. 5th Avenue, 99501, tel: 907-276-6000.* Dinner Mon–Sat (summer), Tues–Sat (winter). On the top floor of the Hotel Captain Cook, this upscale restaurant has a varied menu and some of the best views of the city. Bar. Reservations strongly recommended.

Glacier Brewhouse $$ *737 W. 5th Avenue, 99501, tel: 907-274-2739.* Lunch and dinner daily. Well-prepared food – local seafood and rotisserie-roasted meats – and their own micro-brewed beer; efficient staff. Popular. Reservations recommended.

Gwennies $$$ *4333 Spenard Road, 99517, tel: 907-243-2090.* Breakfast, lunch, dinner daily. This big, family-friendly restaurant is known for its Alaskan-themed décor and large portions. Bar.

Lucky Wishbone $ *1033 E. 5th Avenue, tel: 907-272-3454.* Lunch and dinner Mon–Sat. Hamburgers and fried chicken, and a step back into Anchorage's past. Rarely a long wait for a table.

Moose's Tooth $$ *330 Old Seward Hwy, tel: 907-258-2537.* Lunch and dinner daily. Delicious gourmet pizzas and their own microbrews. Expect a wait. Covered outdoor dining in summer.

Simon & Seafort's $$$$ *420 L Street, 99501, tel: 907-274-3502.* Lunch Mon–Fri, dinner daily. Window tables with views of Cook Inlet. Prime beef and seafood. Bar. Reservations recommended.

Sourdough Mining Company $$$ *5200 Juneau Street, tel: 907-563-2272.* Lunch and dinner daily. A big, Alaskan-themed restaurant where there's rarely a long wait, even for large groups. Family-friendly with burgers, salads, and barbecued meats. Bar.

TALKEETNA

Foraker Restaurant $$$ *Mile 12.5, Talkeetna Spur Road, tel: 907-265-4501 or 888-959-9590.* Breakfast, lunch, and dinner daily. Elegant restaurant noted for creative use of local ingredients.

Talkeetna Roadhouse $$ *Main and C Street, tel: 907-733-1351.* Breakfast, lunch, and light dinner daily (summer), limited hours in winter. Historic roadhouse, popular with Mount McKinley climbers, features home-made soups and fresh baked goods. Beer and wine.

KENAI PENINSULA

KENAI/SOLDOTNA

Charlotte's Bakery, Café, Espresso $ *115 S. Willow Street, Suite 102, Kenai 99611, tel: 907-283-2777.* Breakfast and lunch Mon–Fri. Sandwiches and soups using vegetables from their own garden are served at this bright and cheerful café. Children's menu.

Mykel 's $$$$ *35041 Kenai Spur Hwy, Soldotna 99669, tel: 907-262-4305.* Lunch and dinner daily (summer), Tues–Sat (winter). Innovative and delicious seafood. Bar. Reservations recommended.

HOMER

Boardwalk Fish and Chips $ *4287 Homer Spit Road, tel: 907-235-7749.* Lunch and dinner (summer). Busy place specializing in fish and chips but burgers and hotdogs are also available.

Fat Olives $$ *276 Ohlson Lane, 99603, tel: 907-235-8488.* Lunch and dinner daily. Mediterranean food cooked on a wood-fired oven that is the focal point of the restaurant. Beer and wine.

Fresh Sourdough Express Bakery and Café $$$ *1316 Ocean Drive, 99603, tel: 907-235-7571.* Breakfast, lunch, and dinner daily (summer), breakfast and lunch (spring and fall). Wholesome, fresh ingredients; seafood chowder and reindeer grill as well as an extensive vegetarian/vegan menu. Beer and wine.

Homestead, Homer $$$$ *Mile 8.2 East End Road, 99603, tel: 907-235-8723*. Dinner daily (summer), Wed–Sat (winter). Closed Jan–Mar. Smart restaurant in log cabin setting. Seafood and steaks. Children's menu. Bar. Reservations recommended.

SEWARD

Apollo Restaurant $$ *229 4th Avenue, 99644, tel: 907-224-3092*. Lunch and dinner daily (summer), lunch (winter). This family-friendly place serves Greek and Italian food and local seafood. Beer and wine.

Ray's Waterfront $$$$ *1316 4th Avenue, 99664, tel: 907-224-3816*. Lunch and dinner daily. Large windows overlook the small boat harbor. Seafood and meat menu. Box lunches available. Bar.

KODIAK

Eagle's Nest $$$ *1395 Airport Way, 99615, tel: 907-487-2700*. Breakfast, lunch, dinner daily. Elegant restaurant overlooking river, forest, and mountains. Varied menu offers local seafood. Bar.

Henry's Great Alaskan Restaurant $$ *512 Marine Way, 99516, tel: 907-486-8844*. Lunch and dinner daily. Features reasonably priced seafood, steaks, gourmet hamburgers, and sandwiches. Bar.

King's Diner $ *1941 Mill Bay Road, 99516, tel: 907-486-4100*. Breakfast and lunch daily. Sourdough pancakes make this a breakfast hot spot. Watch through the windows as Bush planes take off.

The Old Powerhouse Restaurant $$$ *516 E. Marine Way 99615, tel: 907-481-1088*. In a renovated building that was once the powerhouse for the city. Fine Japanese cuisine with lovely views of the sea. Reservations recommended for dinner.

PRINCE WILLIAM SOUND

CORDOVA

Ambrosia Restaurant $$ *410 First Street, 99574, tel: 907-424-7175*. Dinner daily (summer). Family restaurant offers seafood, pizza and other Italian dishes. Beer and wine.

Baja Taco $ *Nicholoff Street at the Harbor, 99574, tel: 907-424-5599*. Lunch and dinner daily May–Sept. Fish tacos are the specialty at this converted red school bus. No credit cards.

Killer Whale Café $ *507 First Street, 99574, tel: 907-424-7733*. Breakfast, lunch, dinner Mon–Sat. Fresh food, generous portions.

Lighthouse Inn $ *212 Nicholoff Street, 99574, tel: 907-424-7080*. Breakfast Tues–Sun, lunch and dinner Tues–Sat. Pastries and pizzas baked in wood-fired brick oven. Sticky buns served in the morning.

VALDEZ

Alaska's Bistro $$$ *102 N. Harbor Drive, 99686, tel: 907-835-4447*. Lunch and dinner daily. 'Nouvelle Mediterranean' cuisine features local seafood and pizza. Bar. Reservations recommended.

Alaska Halibut House $ *208 Meals Avenue, 99686, tel: 907-835-2788*. Breakfast, lunch, and dinner daily (summer), lunch and dinner (winter). An inexpensive place to grab a quick, tasty meal.

Mike's Palace Ristorante $$$ *201 N. Harbor Drive, 99686, tel: 907-835-2365*. Lunch and dinner daily. Steak, seafood, and enchiladas in addition to pizza and Italian fare. Beer and wine.

The Pipeline Club $$$ *112 Egan Drive, 99686, tel: 907-835-4444*. Dinner only. This establishment's fine dining menu specializes in steak and seafood. Pool table and indoor golf. Bar. Reservations recommended.

INTERIOR

DENALI

McKinley Creekside Café $$$ *Mile 224 Parks Hwy, 99755, tel: 907-683-2277.* Breakfast, lunch, and dinner daily (summer). Food ranges from burgers and salads to steaks and seafood. They pack sack lunches for the bus ride into the park. Children's menu.

Nenana View Grille $$$ *Mile 238.9 Parks Hwy, 99755, tel: 907-683-8200.* Breakfast, lunch, and dinner May–Sept. Gourmet fare to Alaskan specialties and light meals. Views of the Nenana River through the windows or from the outdoor deck.

Panorama Pizza Pub $$ *Mile 224 Parks Hwy, 99755, tel: 907-683-2623.* Lunch and dinner daily May–Sept. Quick, tasty inexpensive meals. Sack lunches for the bus ride. Children's menu.

FAIRBANKS

Bakery Restaurant $$ *69 College Road, 99701, tel: 907-456-8600.* Breakfast, lunch, and dinner daily. Home-style meals and fresh baked desserts. Children's menu.

L'assiette de Pomegranate $ *414 2nd Avenue, 99701, tel: 907-451-7505.* Breakfast and lunch daily. Bistro-style restaurant features home-made sandwiches, salads, and baked goods. No credit cards.

Pike's Landing $$$$ *4438 Airport Way, 99709, tel: 907-579-6500.* Lunch and dinner daily. Pleasant view of Chena River from a linen-draped table or out on the deck. Varied menu makes this one of Fairbanks's favorite restaurants. Bar. Reservations strongly recommended.

Pump House Restaurant $$$$ *796 Chena Pump Road, 99709, tel: 907-479-8452.* Lunch and dinner daily (summer), dinner daily, and Sunday brunch (winter). Housed in an historic former pump house and decorated with relics from gold-rush days, the long list of regional dishes includes reindeer stew and king crab. Outdoor seating. Bar. Reservations recommended.

The Turtle Club $$$$ *Mile 10, Old Steese Hwy, 99712, tel: 907-457-3883*. Open year-round, this restaurant is a favorite with local people. Limited but delicious menu selections include huge portions of prime rib and seafood. Casual, small, dark dining room. Relatively rowdy bar. Reservations recommended.

Zach's Restaurant $$$$ *1717 University Avenue S., 99709, tel: 907-479-3650*. Breakfast, lunch, and dinner daily. Menu focuses on continental cuisine with Alaskan seafood as the centerpiece. Steaks and lighter meals also available. Bar. Reservations recommended.

THE BUSH

BARROW

Arctic Pizza $$$ *125 Apayauq Street, tel: 907-852-4222*. Lunch and dinner daily. The full menu includes seafood, steaks, and Mexican cuisine. Choose downstairs for family dining, upstairs for views of the Arctic Ocean in a more sophisticated environment.

Pepe's North of the Border Restaurant $$$ *1204 Agvik Street, tel: 907-852-8200*. Breakfast, lunch, and dinner daily. Three dining rooms offer ample portions of Mexican and American food.

NOME

Fat Freddies $$$ *309 Front Street, 99762, tel: 907-443-5899*. Breakfast, lunch, and dinner daily. At the Iditarod finish line, where you can look out over the Bering Sea as you enjoy home-made soups, hamburgers, and other satisfying fare. Bar.

Polar Café $$$ *205 Front Street, 99762, tel: 907-443-5191*. Breakfast, lunch, and dinner daily. Standard meals served at reasonable prices, plus a view of the Bering Sea. Bar. Reservations recommended.